"Leaders get into ministry because they wa
But too often, leadership can lead to burnou
Burn Out, Burn Bright, Jason and Jonathaı
will help you thrive."

Andy Stanley, senior pastor, North Point Ministries

"Navigating the complexity of life and leadership seems to get harder every year. In this book, replete with stories and real-world examples every leader can relate to, Jason and Jonathan offer a practical guide to making it through leadership in a healthy way."

Carey Nieuwhof, bestselling author of *At Your Best*, podcaster,
and founder of TheArtofLeadershipAcademy.com

"Jason and Jonathan have hit the nail on the head in their new book, *Don't Burn Out, Burn Bright.* They address a problem that has been ignored for too long—burnout in leadership—with real, attainable solutions. Thank you for bringing this valuable resource into the leadership world."

Charles Nieman, founder and senior pastor, Abundant Church

"Faced with the demands of life, family, and ministry, pastors are burning out at a seemingly higher rate than ever before. In *Don't Burn Out, Burn Bright,* Jason Young and Jonathan Malm provide spiritual and practical guidelines for pastors struggling with balancing the demands of pastoral leadership with life. Young and Malm provide keen insight into the subtle nuances of perfectionism, control, and boundaries and their impact on the pastoral leader. This book can easily be contextualized across ministry expressions and is a must-read for every pastor in need of striking the balance between life and pastoral leadership."

Dr. Craig L. Oliver Sr., pastor, Elizabeth Baptist Church

"*Don't Burn Out, Burn Bright* achieves a striking balance between idealism and practicality. At a time when leaders—especially ministry leaders—are under pressure like never before, its call to careful circumspection is helpful at any level of responsibility. I hope young leaders in particular heed its advice and follow the path to shining brightly over an entire career."

Dr. Gene Fant, president, North Greenville University

"The journey of providing pastoral leadership is fulfilling, yet many leaders burn out in the process. In *Don't Burn Out, Burn Bright,* Jason and Jonathan provide practical insights to help leaders take a careful inventory of their lives and take the necessary steps to be effective for the long haul. Because of the authors' experience and proximity to leaders, readers are provided with indispensable wisdom to assist them in impacting others and remaining emotionally, mentally, and spiritually vibrant."

Jason Caine, lead campus pastor, Bayside Church, Blue Oaks Campus

"It is tragically ironic that those serving the Prince of Peace and the Good Shepherd are regularly burning out and growing discouraged. Jason Young and Jonathan Malm demonstrate that leaders should expect challenges but not burnout. You will find much wisdom and practical examples in these pages to help you thrive throughout your calling."

Dr. Richard Blackaby, author and president,
Blackaby Ministries International

"Every week, I hear from pastors who are exhausted, ready to quit, or recovering from personal failure. The polarization in our culture and congregations puts a can't-win pressure on those who lead our churches. Mental health challenges are front and center among pastors more than I've ever seen. I'm grateful for the incredibly practical tips found in these pages. The recommended rhythms from Jason and Jonathan are life-giving and will help you regain your joy and passion for people."

Tim Stevens, executive pastor, Willow Creek Community Church

"As a church leader with over forty years in ministry, I can say that *Don't Burn Out, Burn Bright* by Jason and Jonathan is greatly needed for every church leader who wants to go the distance in a healthy and productive way. Their new book delivers practical insights for ministry in a complex and fast-paced world."

Dr. Dan Reiland, executive pastor, 12Stone Church

"What I really love about this book is the unapologetic way it speaks to reality. Most pastors and Christian leaders understand the reality of discouragement and exhaustion. The call to serve our Savior carries the highest honor and the greatest joy, but the demands of ministry can lead to the depths of despair. Every leader should read these words from Jason and Jonathan. They are well crafted, highly practical in application, and written with solutions in mind. They are very encouraging words for which I am most deeply grateful."

Dr. Don Wilton, pastor, First Baptist Church, Spartanburg, SC; preacher,
The Encouraging Word broadcast; author of *Saturdays with Billy*

"One of the great challenges of ministry is learning to manage and cope with the inevitable ups and downs that plague and push us. Resources that are targeted toward keeping leaders motivated and encouraged during challenging times are scarce. Survival through these seasons is best done when we have put mechanisms of prevention from and barriers to discouragement in place. Jason Young and Jonathan Malm have written a life-changing and ministry-saving resource that focuses on preventing burnout and discouragement. I wholeheartedly recommend *Don't Burn Out, Burn Bright* for every leader and pastor. Make the kingdom investment to survive and thrive in life and ministry."

Dr. Charles E. Goodman Jr., senior pastor/teacher,
Tabernacle Baptist Church

"After serving in ministry for forty-four years, I've realized that many fellow pastors never complete the task God set before them. Why? Emotional, mental, spiritual, and physical burnout. Jason and Jonathan have put their years of experience together in this incredible book to encourage you for the long haul."

Sam Davis, associate pastor, First Baptist Church, Spartanburg, SC

DON'T BURN OUT,
BURN BRIGHT

DON'T BURN OUT,
BURN BRIGHT

HOW TO THRIVE IN MINISTRY
FOR THE LONG HAUL

JASON YOUNG AND JONATHAN MALM

BakerBooks

a division of Baker Publishing Group
Grand Rapids, Michigan

Published by Baker Books
a division of Baker Publishing Group
Grand Rapids, Michigan
www.bakerbooks.com

Printed in the United States of America

Library of Congress Cataloging-in-Publication Data
Names: Young, Jason, 1978– author. | Malm, Jonathan, author.
Title: Don't burn out, burn bright : how to thrive in ministry for the long haul / Jason Young and Jonathan Malm.
Description: Grand Rapids, Michigan : Baker Books, a division of Baker Publishing Group, 2023. | Includes bibliographical references.
Identifiers: LCCN 2022044039 | ISBN 9781540902955 (paperback) | ISBN 9781540903242 (casebound) | ISBN 9781493441204 (ebook)
Subjects: LCSH: Church management. | Christian leadership.
Classification: LCC BV652 .Y68 2023 | DDC 254—dc23/eng/20221223
LC record available at https://lccn.loc.gov/2022044039

The authors are represented by the literary agency of The Blythe Daniel Agency, Inc.

Baker Publishing Group publications use paper produced from sustainable forestry practices and post-consumer waste whenever possible.

23 24 25 26 27 28 29   7 6 5 4 3 2 1

CONTENTS

FOREWORD

How have I stayed strong in ministry for over forty years? That's the question Jason and Jonathan asked me to write about for this foreword. My answer ultimately comes down to staying encouraged. Over the years, I've learned that the combination of people, processes, and my own personality can hinder or contribute to success in my life and ministry.

When I first began the journey to plant Bayside Church, I did it kicking and screaming. God and the people around me kept pushing me to start the church, but I had fears. I was afraid to be a pastor. I was afraid to start a church. I was afraid no one would come. I was afraid no one would help. I was afraid to construct a building. I was afraid to raise money. I could have easily felt discouraged before even getting started.

Through each stage of the process, though, God showed me that my fear didn't limit what he was able to accomplish. People showed up. They volunteered. They gave. Families were healed. Communities were impacted. I've seen God's faithfulness as the church became one of the fastest-growing churches in America.

One thing we find abundantly clear in the account of the Israelites in the book of Exodus is that seeing miracles doesn't keep discouragement from creeping in. And I found myself having to battle it at every stage of growth in my ministry.

Maintaining health in ministry for the long haul has been about remembering challenging times and letting those moments turn into hope inside me. You see, hope is a by-product of something you do. Underneath every thriving person, church, business, and relationship is one factor: hope. I had to evaluate what I was doing that would consistently yield hope.

Discouragement precedes destruction. Discouragement drains our energy and pulls us down. But encouragement restores our energy.

I deeply value energy when it comes to leadership. I stay away from things that drain it. Over the years, I've learned I need an intentional game plan because encouragement and energy don't happen accidentally. Practically speaking, I evaluate what will boost energy and keep discouragement at bay. I've noticed patterns in my life. Encouragement comes from seeing people versus noticing people, doing more of what I love, getting away from work more often, riding the highs, embracing the lows, bouncing back after something hard, keeping impact above ego, and passionately loving my family and being present with them. If I can figure out ways to keep my energy up, the by-product is hope. That helps me be in ministry for the long haul.

That's why I'm so excited Jason and Jonathan wrote this book. They understand the importance of energy and hope. I encourage you to lean into the lessons in this book. Let it change you and help you rediscover your impact.

Nothing great happens through you until it happens in you. My hope is that *Don't Burn Out, Burn Bright* will start a change inside you that overflows into every area of your life and leadership. My prayer is that you'll let hope replace fear, energy replace exhaustion, and joy replace dread in your ministry and in your leadership.

Ray Johnston
Founding Senior Pastor, Bayside Church
President, Thrive Communications, Inc.

1 | LEADERSHIP IS EXHAUSTING

Burnout in leadership is not inevitable.

When leaders operate with strength and health, it's like a life-giving fire. It provides warmth, light, and protection for those around it. Strong, healthy leadership provides a sense of belonging, clear vision, and protection from outside threats.

STORY: Jonathan

My grandpa was a Cajun from deep in the swamps of Louisiana. He'd had a hard life. His leg was stiffened from polio at an early age. His brother had been murdered in a bar fight and lay on their kitchen table for days until the family could do a proper burial. He'd worked in oil his whole life, and he loved getting his hands dirty on his property.

I was and am the opposite. We couldn't relate on a lot of shared emotions or interests. The one thing, though, that connected us was building fires in his woodstove.

13

The first time my grandpa had me help him stack the logs, I found it annoying. He was so precise with the way he wanted me to build the fire:

Some of the newspaper had to be bundled tightly so it wouldn't burn too quickly.

Some had to be loosely crumpled so it caught. (That had to be in the front of the woodstove.)

There had to be a big log in the back to provide lasting heat.

There had to be twigs beneath the other logs that could catch the flame from the newspaper.

And there had to be just the right amount of space between the logs so air could flow through but heat could also build and combust.

As a six-year-old, I felt this was all tedious and unnecessary. But when the ritual was complete and I held the match to the paper, my eyes lit up as I saw everything working together just as my grandpa had explained. The wood caught quickly, and the heat it produced was satisfying.

That was our thing. I was always the first to volunteer to build the fire, and he kept correcting my technique for as long as he was alive.

I still get a bit smug when I see others try to build a fire. I even feel a bit superior when someone uses starter logs—it feels like cheating to me.

Building a fire is a sacred art form for me. It connects me to my grandpa, but I also know the power of a well-built fire. There's life in a well-lit, well-contained fire.

Fire is a beautiful picture of leadership. We've all known people who have tried, figuratively, to douse their leadership in lighter fluid. They want to infuse energy and impact into their job, so they add a bunch of hype, hoping that will do the trick. They burn hot and bright, but they quickly burn out. There's no sustaining the fire.

We've also seen people whose leadership passion is a smoldering coal—they are barely hanging on and wallowing in discouragement.

Good leadership is like a good fire. And just like building a good fire, good leadership requires the right elements put together in the right way.

Here's the good news: We believe you have all the right elements to be a healthy, high-capacity leader. We want to help you assemble them so you burn brightly. There are a lot of things that would seek to put your fire out, but we believe it's possible to keep the fire going.

We know you signed up to lead because you wanted to burn brightly despite the obstacles you would face. You didn't sign up because it would be easy.

You love the challenge of leadership. You love the high stakes of leadership—especially in ministry, where eternities hang in the balance.

The problem is, leadership is exhausting.

We googled that phrase—"leadership is exhausting"—and over 165 million results showed up. It doesn't even seem like there are 165 million leaders in the first place. Yet that's how much of an issue this exhaustion is.

It doesn't matter if you're working in ministry or in an industry. Leading other people can be tiring.

One thing to remember about leadership exhaustion is that it's a slow road to get there. You might not even realize you're getting tired as you go along. And if you aren't careful, exhaustion can lead to burnout.

That burnout is like a snap. It's like a broken bone. Burnout can feel like a break in its devastation, but not in the way that it happens. It isn't a sudden thing.

Just like a broken bone, though, healing from burnout takes a long time. There's no swift bouncing back. In fact, recovering from burnout takes at least as long as it took to get there, and sometimes longer. And some leaders are never the same after it.

It's not like any leaders are intentionally doing things that lead to their exhaustion. Nobody looks in the mirror in the morning and says, "Today's the perfect day for unhealthy decisions."

Still, those decisions happen. One step at a time. One choice. One compromise. One time of taking the easy way out. One shortcut. One yes that should have been no. It's so easy to take small steps toward exhaustion.

If we were to examine our motives for these steps, we would find they're often rooted in things like

- addiction to motion
- insecurity
- fear of rejection
- fear of failure
- fear of irrelevance
- procrastination
- pride
- laziness

We're all at risk for exhaustion in leadership because we all have internal dysfunction. In fact, think about the greatest leader you've ever worked under. They were struggling with one or a combination of these dysfunctions, but they still found how to lead in a healthy way. It is possible.

STORY: Jason

I experienced exhaustion when I worked under a high-level leader. When he promoted me and told me he wanted me to work for him, I didn't calculate the time and energy this new role would require. In a couple of years, I found myself exhausted.

As my leader, he was partly responsible for my exhaustion. But the bigger responsibility rested on my shoulders. I tried to do more than I could and for longer than I should have. I pushed to prove to myself (and to him) that I was worthy of the promotion instead of simply focusing on adding value. You see, he already knew I was worthy of the promotion, but my insecurity didn't let me believe that. I refused to ask for help. I felt like I always had to be "on."

When I look back on the experience of leading in that organization, I see how many times I showed up to all service times when I should have probably stayed home. One time I had bronchitis and I was still there. The fault was my own. Nobody was pushing me to work in spite of illness. Yet I felt such a weight of responsibility to execute my job and never have an off day.

When I'd first begun working in the organization, I loved leading. But two years later, without my realizing it, I disliked it. I was in the opposite place from where I'd wanted to end up two years prior. I'd drifted there and found myself in survival mode.

The by-products of this exhaustion were obvious. I was

- discouraged
- lacking energy
- no longer caring as deeply for people
- no longer caring about some things
- not as creative
- experiencing brain fog
- shorter with my family
- unwilling to try new things
- unwilling to reach out to people
- slacking on my time with God

The last one was the most devious. I should have been drawing strength and energy from the Lord, but instead, my exhaustion kept me away from him. It touched every area of my life, but I had dug myself into such a hole that I felt like I couldn't let people know. I acted as if everything was under control, and that in itself was exhausting.

Hiding made me try harder, but I didn't really care about what I was doing. I just kept up the ruse so nobody knew.

I wish I could say I bounced back, but "bounce" is the worst word I could choose. It took me time and energy to crawl out of exhaustion and back into health again.

Hustle Culture

Over the last few decades, a culture has sprung up in most of the Western world. It's a hustle culture that celebrates working hard as the ultimate virtue. It's an unhealthy form of entrepreneurship, and it's become so pervasive because the internet has made it possible for anyone to become an entrepreneur. Whether we're a social media influencer, manage an Etsy shop, or have some other side hustle, we are doing some form of entrepreneurism. And the hustle culture has made us believe that we have to post every day, sell just one more product, gain more followers . . . It's a perpetual "more, more, more" mentality. We never seem to arrive, and the cycle leads toward burnout.

First of all, churches should be speaking into this topic because it's fostering many unhealthy habits in our society. Second, we have to identify that this culture has infiltrated ministry. This isn't just a worldly mentality. It has infected the church.

Most church staff members have a side hustle of some type. And many pastors feel the pressure to become social media influencers, though they would say it's for the purpose of ministry. Even megachurch culture has become a reflection of this hustle-culture mentality: "We need more people in the seats because each person represents an eternal soul." That's true, but if you don't approach that concept in a healthy way, it can become a rallying point for hustle culture within the church. That "one more soul" can become a relentless goal instead of something we trust in the hands of God.

Our goal should be health, not hustle.

Now, that isn't to say hustling is bad. Seasons of intense, hard work are a part of any high-performing leadership role. The problem is when hustle becomes a lifestyle instead of a short-term sprint to accomplish a goal. We can't sprint a marathon. Neither can we sprint our entire leadership life. We have to understand how to pace ourselves.

Another way this hustle culture works itself out is the idea that we can't have a bad day. We always have to be "on." We have to appear that we've got everything together, we have to put on a smile, and we have to do our best 100 percent of the time.

In business, this is called "emotional labor." It's the barista who puts on a cheery face each morning even when they're discouraged. We applaud people who can do this and look down on people who can't. That isn't to say every emotion should be out there for the world to see, but neither should we walk around 24/7 with a fake smile plastered on our faces.

Some of this feeling of always having to be "on" is self-inflicted. But a lot of it is a reflection of the shift in our culture. Deep down, we're all worried about making the mistake that absolutely ruins us. Maybe we tweet something without fully thinking through the ramifications of what we're saying, and a powerful interest group takes offense. Or we say something from the stage on a bad day, and that sound bite gets around the whole world, with news media demanding a statement. We've all seen the consequences of small mistakes within the church, and they can be devastating. They're just another reflection of this unhealthy leadership culture that has wormed its way into our everyday lives.

Should it be that way? No.

Unfortunately, this reality of hustle culture will always be an expectation placed on high-level leaders until culture changes. And that likely won't be for a few more decades. Many have identified how unhealthy the concept can be, but few have made any changes to fix it. It'll be a slow recovery, just as it slowly crept into culture.

Here's the good news, though: Hustle culture doesn't have to take you out. You can be healthy for the long haul. That's the goal, and it's possible to get there. But how?

Take stock of where you are. Do you find yourself heading toward exhaustion or, even worse, toward burnout?

If you were to rate yourself on a scale from 1 to 10—1 being exhausted and 10 being energetic and healthy in your leadership— where would you be? We created a leadership health assessment in appendix A. Take a moment to identify just where you land on that scale.

If you're at a level 1, you're probably either burned out or one small mistake away from it. We encourage you to get a counselor. There are many out there to help you recover, but you need to be realistic and realize it's a long road to recovery.

This book isn't really about burnout. The market is saturated with books about burnout recovery, yet burnout is higher than ever. We want to help you stay far away from it. We believe you can follow the principles in this book to help you get healthy if you've found yourself in a place of burnout. But the best thing you can do is get to a place of healthy, high-capacity leadership and maintain it for life.

If you're at a 2 or 3, we believe we can get you back to a place of health, energy, and functionality. And the best news is, you won't even need to start over somewhere else. That's one of the temptations when you're exhausted in ministry. It's easy to think starting over will fix the problem. But it won't. The thing that made you valuable to your current organization will be expected at the new one. And the bigger issue—your unreasonable expectations of yourself and your unhealthy habits—will carry over to the new organization. You don't need to start new. You need to get healthy and break the cycle of the things that were leading to exhaustion.

How to Ramp Up Your Health

If you find yourself on the lower end of the spectrum of health in leadership, there are a few steps to take.

1. Evaluate where you are.

Take a break from the hustle. Give yourself some space to become a bit more self-aware and acknowledge your reality. What are you feeling? Do you feel unhealthy? Do you feel exhausted? Evaluate what's going on in your heart and in your leadership.

Are you showing some of these warning signs of unhealthy leadership?

- Feeling discouraged
- Lacking energy
- No longer caring for people
- No longer caring about some things
- Feeling less creative
- Experiencing brain fog

- Responding more aggressively to family
- Unwilling to try new things
- Unwilling to reach out to people
- Slacking on time with God
- No longer brilliant at the basics (the things you expect others to do too)

Take some time to pray about this. Ask God to show you where you are in this journey toward health.

2. Admit and accept where you are.

One of the worst things you can do in leadership is deny your current reality. Problems don't go away. They fester, grow, and eat away at the health of any organization until it ultimately crumbles. The same is true for the lives of individuals.

Admitting where you are is one of the first things therapists have you do when you sit down with them. And admitting sounds easy, but it isn't. If it was so easy, you would have already done it.

If you're unhealthy, truly one of the best things you can do is go to a counselor and admit where you find yourself. There's value in counseling, because a counselor is someone who cares about you but is less connected emotionally to your success. It can be hard to admit you're unhealthy to people like bosses, coworkers, employees, family, or even friends. You don't want them to worry. You don't want them to think less of you. You don't want them to start looking for your replacement. A counselor can help you talk through the reality of your situation without making it about themselves.

But if you're against counseling or feel like you can't make time for it, find someone you can trust. Find someone who cares about you but doesn't have an emotional stake in your success, and talk things through with them. Let them help you reclaim a better picture of and for your life.

Dr. Tim Elmore, generational expert and leadership author, says,

Change doesn't happen until you:

1. know enough that you are able to,
2. care enough that you want to, or
3. hurt enough that you have to.[1]

3. Give yourself permission to move forward toward health.

Don't beat yourself up if you find yourself in an unhealthy place. Remove the guilt and shame from the equation. Shame tries to keep you stuck, but freedom propels you forward.

A scene in the show *Yellowstone* creates a beautiful picture of this. Kevin Costner's character, John, owns a ranch. His grandson has come to live with him for a bit, and John tells him to go inside the house and choose a donut before he goes to school. After a few minutes, John goes into the house and sees his grandson staring at the donuts, seemingly unable to make a decision. The boy says, "I want to get the biggest one, but I can't figure out which one that is."

John suggests that he take them all off the plate and line them up.

The grandson replies, "I can do that?"

John says, "Grandson, you can do whatever you want when you're here."[2]

Isn't that just what a good grandfather says to his grandkids? It's like he gives them the keys to his kingdom: "My house is your house. Make yourself at home and do whatever you want."

That's the mentality we're trying to give you here. We want you to wander through your soul and take inventory of what's in there. So rearrange things. Explore. Take ownership of what's there.

Denial keeps you as a guest in your own home.

More importantly, we want you to invite the Holy Spirit into your situation in the same way. Let *him* rearrange and reorder things in your heart. Let *him* take stock of what's in there.

That's what David did. In Psalm 139:23–24, he says, "Search me, O God, and know my heart; test my thoughts. Point out anything you find in me that makes you sad, and lead me along the path of everlasting life" (TLB).

Once you have permission to analyze your soul and rearrange some things, imagine yourself a year from now. Describe what would make that vision remarkable. What's in the way of that? What do you need to make that day happen?

We're willing to believe that everything you just imagined is fully possible.

4. Create a circle of trusted people to help you move forward.

Evaluate the people in your life. Use the following list of eleven types of people to see what you're missing. Lean on them and let them know what you're working toward. Burning bright means bringing things to light; just make sure you're confiding in the right people.

1. *Clarifier:* someone who asks helpful and difficult questions. It's easy for us to assume that everyone knows what we're talking about. Clarifiers make sure that happens.
2. *Specialist:* someone who provides precision focus. These people keep the conversation moving toward the intended target.
3. *Challenger:* someone who implores us to act boldly. We might be tempted to leave these people out of the mix, but they bring a lot of energy and direction to the conversation.

These are the people who will help us see the viability of a solution by encouraging action.

4. *Creator:* someone who brings an idea into existence. Creators will help craft workable plans of action from a conversation that might have included few actionable points.

5. *Connector:* someone who leads us to other people. We all need connectors in our lives. They have the ability to size up a situation and identify others who might be able to make a contribution.

6. *Wise Elder:* someone who lends learned experience. It's easy to overlook these people, but they make an incredible contribution to the conversation and provide a viewpoint others don't have.

7. *Friend:* someone who shares life's journey without judgment. These are the people who love us without regard for our accomplishments or positions. These people know us deeply and accept us freely. They stick with us.

8. *Strategist:* someone who maps out steps for our vision. These people are able to create step-by-step simplicity from complex data and conversations. They will help make sure the project has a path to success.

9. *Dreamer:* someone who motivates us to dream without fear. There's a little dreamer in all of us, but these people have a unique ability to see the future and motivate us to go there.

10. *Coach:* someone who builds out our strengths. Coaches correct us when we're performing incorrectly and encourage us when we are losing energy.

11. *Pastor:* someone who can provide spiritual guidance through life. Pastors or spiritual mentors are able to provide insight from a unique perspective.

5. *Get freedom from the symptoms that led you to exhaustion or burnout.*

There are ten key things that lead people toward exhaustion in leadership:

- perfectionism
- constant need for approval
- need for control
- ego and pride
- lack of values
- addictions or vices
- difficult relationships
- incessant hurry (accomplishment, distraction, motion)
- wounds that haven't been healed
- spiritual shallowness

Throughout the rest of this book, we'll be exploring the flip side of these ideas, giving you building blocks for freedom and renewed energy in your leadership.

6. *Draw a mental line in the sand, stating that from this point forward you will move toward burning bright in a healthy way.*

Today is the day it all turns around. Today is the day you identify both what should be and what could be. Today is the day you reimagine what it would look like to be the healthiest version of yourself—the day you imagine what it would look like to stand up in front of people and not feel like you have to hide a piece of yourself.

What's your original vision of what leadership should look like? Leadership is likely not quite what you thought it would be when you first got into it, but there's a good chance *something realistic* attracted you to it. Let's get to the thing that attracted you to leadership in the first place. We won't be naive, but we will be hopeful in the way we approach it.

Back when Michael Jordan was playing basketball, he negotiated a unique clause into his contracts. It was dubbed a "For the Love of the Game" clause. Essentially, it prevented his team managers from keeping him from playing basketball in the off-season, for exhibition games, or for any other purpose (which team managers often did). Michael Jordan loved the game of basketball so much that he didn't want anything to stand in the way of him getting to enjoy the purity of it.

Imagine if you felt that way about leadership again. Imagine if you were so in love with the "game" of leadership that you didn't let anything stand in your way.

That's what burning bright can look like, and we believe you can get there again.

STORY: Kevin Thompson, Married Life Pastor at Bayside Church, Sacramento, California

I got a wake-up call. When I went to my grandmother's funeral and felt no emotion, I knew something was wrong. It was what made me finally realize that for the last five years of ministry I had been heading toward burnout.

For those five years, I had felt so guilty for not being able to figure out what was wrong with me. I'd hacked my way to avoiding all the "burnout indicators" that I'd heard about. I had my Sabbath day of rest and my group of people, and my schedule was good. I thought studying burnout would be enough to keep me from it, but it wasn't.

To recover, I got counseling. I began a season of personal reflection. It led me to realizing that leadership is indeed exhausting, and the only way I would survive was to train. I began seeing things like an athlete does.

Everyone knows that being a professional athlete is exhausting. No matter how well the best tennis or soccer players train, at some point they will experience cramping and be unable to compete. No one questions their toughness or ability in those situations. They take time off, recover, and then play again. Yet for some reason, in leadership we convince ourselves that we can avoid exhaustion. But maybe the better way is to embrace that at times we will need seasons of recovery.

2 | EMBRACE IMPERFECT

The goal isn't perfection; it's effectiveness.

We all want to be part of the perfect ministry and to be the perfect leader. But perfect isn't possible. And an overemphasis on this impossible standard will begin to destroy our ability to lead effectively.

We know perfection is impossible and perfectionism is unhealthy. This isn't a new idea. Still, there's something about high-capacity leaders in ministry . . . We still reach for perfection.

Chris Thurman, a Christian psychologist, says,

> Perfectionism is the destructive belief that we can be equal to God. God is all-knowing, all-powerful, and everywhere at once. When we embrace perfectionism, we think we should have been all-knowing and seen that our actions wouldn't have worked out. Or we should have been all-powerful and done everything perfectly. Or we should have been everywhere at once and fixed everything.[1]

We can't be perfect, and as Thurman suggests, our attempt at perfection is actually us fancying ourselves in the same position as God. That's extremely unfair to ourselves and way too much pressure.

Still, it does feel at times like our role as believers is trying to push us toward perfection. Consider the verses that say, "Be holy, because I am holy," found in both the Old and the New Testament (Lev. 19:2; 1 Pet. 1:16). Doesn't that feel like a call to perfection?

Well, yes, technically, but we also know that we were freed from perfection because Jesus gave his perfection to us. So for our purposes, holiness is about being set apart for the work of God—not us being perfect but embracing Jesus's perfection.

Perfection isn't possible. Either it's a ghost in the woods that you'll never even know if you catch, or it's a standard you saw somewhere else that you are trying to emulate.

And it's a relentless standard, because even if you were somehow able to achieve the greatest thing ever accomplished in the history of humanity, you would still be dissatisfied, because it could always be better. Or, worse, imagine you've achieved the standard of perfection you identified in someone else, and you're just a copy of them. You aren't doing what you were called to do, what you were set apart to do—what you were called to be holy to accomplish.

Perfection is impossible, but that's actually an opportunity for you. There are actually benefits you can experience for your leadership when you're willing to embrace imperfection instead of reaching for perfection. You can actually increase your leadership capacity by embracing the following truths:

1. Ministry is imperfect.
2. Your leadership is imperfect.
3. Your team is imperfect.

Ministry Is Imperfect

Did you hear the story of the pastor who finally built the perfect church? Unfortunately, he couldn't attend, because it wouldn't have been perfect anymore if he was in the building.

STORY: Jonathan

We had just finished filming testimony videos at the church where I worked. I'd been tasked to reach out to five families and collect the stories of how God had worked in their lives through their involvement in our ministry. I scheduled the families and devoted an entire day to interviewing them, editing their stories, and creating short videos we could put on our website and show during the service.

I presented the videos in our staff meeting, and one of our pastoral care team members spoke up. "Well . . . we probably shouldn't show that last video. I've been counseling with them, and they're barely hanging on by a thread. We don't want to celebrate their transformation if their marriage implodes in the next couple of months."

That sounded good in theory, but if we approached ministry that way, we would never show anyone's testimony. We're all a few unwise decisions away from ruining all the progress the Holy Spirit has made in our lives. Thankfully, our pastor understood this fact too, and we showed all five videos. And good news: that couple is still serving the Lord.

Ministry is inherently imperfect because we're working with people. We can't control what people will do. All we can do is help them take small steps toward Jesus; we can't "fix them." That's the Holy Spirit's job.

Along with that imperfection is the truth that we don't have the resources to do everything well. Either we don't have enough money and people to accomplish all the goals, or we have so much money

31

and so many people that we don't have the emotional energy or leadership capacity to use them all effectively. (Don't you wish that was your problem?)

Ministry will always be imperfect and incomplete. We can't do all of it. If we're trying to do everything and trying to do it all well, we will always be frustrated. In fact, we'll probably operate at a lower capacity than we should because we're splitting our focus too much.

Think of it like a cheetah in those nature documentaries. The cheetah approaches a herd, ready to eat. It sneaks up, and when it begins the chase, the herd scatters. In that moment, the cheetah must decide on one target; if it tries to chase every potential meal, it will catch none of them. It's only in the targeted, intentional chase that the cheetah succeeds.

The same is true for your ministry. You can't hope to do much effectively if you're aiming at too many goals. Effective leadership in ministry requires choosing a specific target and putting your attention and energy toward that. (Hint: Your target likely should be the vision God gave you when you started on this road toward leadership, or the vision God gave the person you lead under.)

Set a targeted goal, decide what standard of excellence is good enough, then aim your leadership energy toward that.

Craig Groeschel, the pastor of the largest church in America, says that his aim is to get something to the 80 percent mark. If he can get it there, that's good enough. The final 20 percent requires too much energy, which he could devote to other areas.[2]

In business, the concept of minimum viable product (MVP) is often used as a metric for knowing when a product is done. The MVP is when the product effectively accomplishes the goal it was created to accomplish. This concept keeps businesses from continually adding bells and whistles that don't actually enhance their core product, instead adding cost, delay, and too much organizational energy to it.

When you've created your MVP, you ship it. You can improve it later based on customer feedback, though usually you'll discover the improvements weren't as necessary as you were tempted to believe when creating the product.

The 80 percent rule and the MVP concept apply to ministry over and over. As circumstances and capacity change, you evaluate what's possible and necessary, then make adjustments.

STORY: Jonathan

My pastor, Daniel Villarreal, made a difficult decision during the season of COVID protocols that perfectly highlights the idea of a minimum viable product in ministry. It was a season when many churches were seeing a fraction of their attendance. Giving was down, and volunteer numbers were way down.

After one particularly disastrous Sunday when half of the volunteers scheduled to serve that week came down with the virus, he made a decision. He would be cutting the Sunday morning livestream, reducing the number of band members on stage, and reducing the capacity of the children's ministry. Instead, those who could attend only online would have a special service created for them midweek via Zoom.

It was a bold move, but Daniel had seen the results of people trying to maintain the status quo in that difficult season. Friends of his were burning out. Their church doors were closing. And he was unwilling to see that happen for his church. Instead, this change kept volunteers from being burned out and allowed the team to focus on the core goals of ministry.

The church is now thriving, team members haven't burned out, and Daniel is still leading from a healthy, high-capacity place.

Your Leadership Is Imperfect

If you're reading this book, there's a good chance your goal is to be the perfect leader. You probably consume many books each year to learn best practices, leadership theory, effective ministry . . .

Can we get rid of that notion real quickly? You won't be the perfect leader. In fact, striving too hard to be the perfect leader can be a disaster both for you and for your team.

When we strive too hard to be the perfect leader, we will always fall short. Yet the temptation to appear perfect will remain. We'll chase the image of perfection. That creates a chasm between who we actually are and who we want people to perceive us to be. That image of perfection creates a mask we hide behind. Masks turn into more deceptions. And all these deceptions can sometimes turn into moral failure, because we become so used to hiding who we really are that it's easy to live two separate lives. Those who are experts at hiding their true selves are the ones who engage in sexual sin, lying, embezzling money, manipulating their congregations . . . The list goes on.

Maybe you won't be victim to one of those moral failures that turn into national headlines, but hiding behind a mask of perfection will guarantee unhealthy leadership for you. More than that, though, it will negatively impact those you lead. The truth is, people aren't attracted to perfect leaders. We're attracted to effective, humble leaders, even embracing their flaws as something endearing when those flaws are accompanied by humility.

We're attracted to imperfect people because they give us hope that we can be effective too. We're actually drawn more to imperfect people than to those who seem to have it all together. When someone in our lives seems to have everything all together, there's no role for us in their life. We want to be needed, so their imperfection gives us space to exist. Imperfect leaders, weirdly enough, provide a sense of safety for those they lead.

Churches have gained a reputation, whether deserved or not, for expecting perfection from their people. It's a reputation for behavior modification, which doesn't give room for mistakes, morally or otherwise. Because of this reputation, it's in the back of most people's minds that perfection is required, especially if excellence is valued highly in their church. When we give off the air of perfection, we unintentionally reinforce this idea in people's minds.

STORY: Jason

I've been guilty of trying to be a perfect leader, to the detriment of my influence. In fact, I've been told a few times that the unreasonably high expectations I place on myself get adopted by those I lead. They see how hard I am on myself when I don't do things perfectly, and that unintentionally communicates to those I lead that they should be perfect. Though I might not show it to them, they think I'll be just as disappointed with them if they fail as I am with myself when I fail.

That's nothing I'd ever communicate, and I'm not even sure I *am* that hard on people, but my striving for perfection can come across that way.

Your Team Is Imperfect

Within the slew of superhero movies made in the last two decades, you probably missed a lesser-known but well-cast movie called *Mystery Men*. It stars a lot of heavy hitters like Ben Stiller, Greg Kinnear, William H. Macy, and Geoffrey Rush. What we love about this movie is it's the ultimate misfit movie.

When Champion City gets taken over by the villainous Casanova Frankenstein, only Captain Amazing has any hope of stopping him.

Unfortunately, Captain Amazing gets taken and imprisoned by the villain, leaving a group of second-rate heroes working to save the city:

The Blue Raja, who hurls forks at the bad guys

Shoveler, who fights with a shovel

Mr. Furious, who gets very, very angry (not extra strong, just extra angry)

Invisible Boy, who can be invisible but only when nobody's watching

Sphinx, who's terribly mysterious (nobody knows what his powers are)

As any good ensemble hero movie does, the story highlights how each person's seemingly meager power comes together with the others' in order to save Champion City. It's a terribly ridiculous movie, but it's one of Jonathan's favorites.

While *Mystery Men* is an extreme example of this movie genre, we all love stories about misfits saving the world. It's fun to see how each person's unique ability contributes to the success of the mission.

The disciples were a lot like that. Jesus was perfect, but he chose fishermen, a tax collector, a zealot . . . and we aren't quite sure what the other guys did. Yet they came together, empowered by Jesus and then the Holy Spirit, and began a worldwide movement of evangelism. More important than who they were was who they were with.

The same is true for your team. They won't be perfect. Even Jesus's team was filled with highly flawed individuals. Yet with a leader who values the strengths of the individuals on their team, they can accomplish great things.

Unfortunately, as leaders—especially perfectionistic leaders—we have a tendency to focus on the things we don't have instead of the things we do. We focus on our lack.

Every winter season, a photo circulates on social media of football fans covered in snow, beers frozen over, huddled under blankets to watch their teams battle it out on the field. Inevitably, we see many pastors posting that same picture, with a caption similar to "If only the church had people as committed as this, imagine what we could accomplish."

The thing is, the pastors sharing this probably already do have people as committed as that. Sure, maybe it's not the two hundred people who attend their church, but what about those four or five who are there every time the doors open? Perhaps those four or five are enough, and the pastor simply needs to value their contribution and put them to work on things that truly matter. After all, simply sitting in the seats of church every time the doors open isn't really the mission, right?

The weird thing about leadership is that if you focus on what you don't have, you often miss the people you do have. Consider the parable of the talents in Matthew 25:14–30. Who was the servant who did the least? The one who felt like he was given the least. Yet the master considered him responsible for making the most of what he had been entrusted with. The servant focused on what he lacked, and then what he did have was taken from him and given to the ones who had put the talents they were entrusted with to work for the benefit of the master.

Could it be that God has already sent you everything you need to accomplish the purpose he has given you as a leader?

You say, "But, Jason and Jonathan, you don't know what I'm working with in my ministry. It would be a miracle if the people could accomplish the huge vision I've been given."

Well, consider this: the miracles Jesus performed always used what was on hand at the time. When he turned water into wine, he used the jugs that were there and filled them with water. When he healed the blind man, he used spit and dirt to create mud. In the feeding of the four thousand and the five thousand, he used the food that was already there. It wasn't *what* the people had at the time; it was *who* they had. Jesus always used something simple that seemed completely unrelated to the mission at hand. But in the hands of God, even simple things can be used for miracles.

No, your team won't be perfect. But they'll be perfect for the mission God has given you. That's perhaps the only perfection attainable to you.

The key to enlisting your band of misfits for the mission is to appreciate what they bring to the table and be sure they're focused on the core goal. Ask yourself, *How can we accomplish our core goal with what we have?* If you aren't constantly bringing the vision back to the core goal, your team will chase things that ultimately don't matter.

In the sci-fi book *Shadow of the Hegemon* by Orson Scott Card, there's a fun scene in which a nun is on the phone with an administrator of a college. She's lying to the administrator in order to find some information, and her friend who's sitting with her confronts her about lying as a nun.

Her response is, "It isn't lying to tell a bureaucrat whatever story it takes to get him to do his job properly. . . . If he does his job properly, he'll understand the purpose of the rules and therefore know when it is appropriate to make exceptions."[3]

This is a silly story, and we certainly aren't recommending you lie to your team to get them to do what you want them to. But it illustrates the flaws in bureaucracy. The structure of bureaucracy tends to focus most on not making mistakes, not innovating, and passing the responsibility on to other departments in order to accomplish those first two objectives. Consequently, members of bureaucracy are quite bad at doing their actual jobs and instead strive for perfection in documentation and other things that aren't their core objective.

The same is often true for teams. We tend to strive for perfection in things that aren't actually what we're supposed to be there for. Especially if we feel like our flaws will get us in trouble.

When we don't embrace the misfits in our organizations, we create an environment that celebrates not making mistakes but also not innovating and passing off responsibility to other people. Team members are more worried about checking off boxes than using their unique intelligence and abilities to accomplish the overall goal of the organization. And team members who don't feel safe resort to behaviors that maintain the status quo.

STORY: Jason

I once worked for a pastor who had all his team members fill out anonymous surveys about him. The goal was to help him grow as a leader, and the survey was intended to be a safe way we could tell him things he needed to know.

He was a great leader. But one time in a meeting, he mentioned something I had written in my survey, and he was directing the comment at me. It felt like he was singling me out, leading me to believe he'd figured out that I was the one who had left that comment.

Can you imagine I no longer felt safe filling out those surveys?

Obviously, I related to the fact that he tracked my response back to me. It's a natural tendency for someone to guess who wrote each comment, because context might help them justify that comment or even explain why the change the person suggested wasn't necessary.

Still, I felt unsafe, so I stopped filling out the surveys. One day the pastor asked me why, which was even more suspicious since he shouldn't have known it was me if the surveys were anonymous.

That season taught me that if you don't make people feel safe in your ministry, they'll either leave or adapt to survive. They'll hide things from you and just do what they think will make you happy, not giving their own energy to actually make things better.

Once again we'll say that you won't be a perfect leader. Trying to be actually puts your team at a deficit. But the same is true when you expect perfection from them. You create an unsafe environment that more often resembles bureaucracy than an innovative, effective team.

Embracing imperfection in your team can actually empower the group to accomplish the goals.

Improving

Now, don't make the mistake of thinking this chapter is celebrating incompetence or mediocrity. We believe strongly in the power of excellence. (It's one whole chapter in our book *The Come Back Effect*.) The difference is between perfection and constant improvement.

If you strive for perfection, you'll never hit it and you'll always be frustrated. But when the goal is improvement, you can actually see progress and have something worth celebrating.

Allow for mistakes. Then use them as a chance to get better with your team. Don't celebrate the mistake; rather, celebrate the opportunity the imperfection gives you: a chance to learn and improve.

Choose clear measurements that indicate whether you're being effective in your mission as a ministry. Choose healthy measurements, not superficial things or goals that don't clearly tie in with the mission.

When you see improvement in the results, celebrate the progress. Plant a flag in the ground that commemorates the success. Get the team cookies. Design a shirt. Hold a pizza party. Do something to celebrate improvement, then move toward the next goal.

The beautiful thing about improving from weekend to weekend is that you get fifty-two times per year to do it. Even small improvements yield huge results at the end of a year.

Remember, perfection is unattainable, and that's actually a good thing. Jesus doesn't want a perfect church; otherwise he'd do everything himself. He's the only one who is perfect. But he chose flawed vessels to partner with him to accomplish the extraordinary.

STORY: Daniel Villarreal, Pastor at Grace Avenue Church, San Antonio, Texas

My wife had a high-risk pregnancy, so we had weekly appointments with the doctor. At thirty-two weeks, the doctor told us we weren't leaving the hospital until my wife delivered. During the ten days we were stuck waiting for my daughter to arrive, team members came to the hospital for meetings and to organize what needed to be done while I was gone.

When it was finally time for the delivery, things went crazy. My wife's body began to shut down, so I had a very premature baby in one wing and a potentially dying wife in another. I had a meeting with the staff and pastor team, and I told them, "From here forward, you're leading the team. My wife and I are out for a while, so you'll be handling the ministry of the church throughout the week."

I arranged to have pastors—friends—I trusted cover the pulpit, then I had to trust my teams to do the rest. They understood my heart. They took it upon themselves to take ownership of the vision and the mission. And the result was that when my wife was healthy and I returned, the church was in a stronger place than before this all happened.

I had rest and focus because my staff lifted my arms. This is why you build a team.

3 | KNOW YOU'RE ENOUGH

One spark is enough to start a blaze.

Just like one small spark can start a destructive forest fire, one small spark can also create life-giving momentum. It can light up excitement for a cause. It can lead an organization to great things. It can give people vision and purpose.

We believe you can be that spark.

STORY: Jason

I was in California one time while one of the frequent forest fires was raging off in the distance. It was 5:00 in the morning, and I could see the red blaze from the fires lighting up the darkened sky. As I saw that massive amount of power, it was incredible to think that it had all started from a single, seemingly insignificant spark.

Insecurity whispers that you aren't enough, and it can eat away at your energy to lead. But in order to maintain healthy, high-capacity leadership, you need to have a strong inner sense that you are enough.

But how do you know you're enough? Like, really know? Three factors play into this:

1. The people you surround yourself with
2. The way you compare yourself with others
3. Having an accurate picture of yourself

The People You Surround Yourself With

When humanity looks back on the great atrocities of history, this question always comes up: Why didn't someone do something to stop the people who perpetrated these evils?

In every instance, we see a narcissistic leader surrounded by people who praise the leader at every turn. That's a consistent trait of people who make the most dramatic changes in the world: They're surrounded by yes-men and yes-women. These yes-people treat the leader like they can do no wrong and don't have the backbone to stand up to the leader when it's clear they're doing evil.

This is extremely unhealthy, and you see that it's true in the way these evil men and women burn out in brilliant blazes of ugliness.

Proverbs 27:6 talks about how unhealthy it is when we surround ourselves with people who praise and flatter us at every turn: "Wounds from a friend can be trusted, but *an enemy multiplies kisses*" (emphasis added). King Solomon talks about these types of flatterers as enemies. First, though, he mentions another type of person: the friend who wounds.

Now, human nature is to think of these two people as being on opposite ends of the spectrum: The one who flatters or the critic.

The yes-person or the one who always challenges us and doesn't think we're anything special.

Our nature as leaders is to surround ourselves with one of these two types of people. Either we want people who tell us how awesome we are, or we want people who constantly bring up areas where we can improve. This tendency partially springs from our need for approval. We listen to advisers and friends to make sure we're doing well. When the flatterers tickle our ears, we feel good. Or when the critics tell us what's wrong, we know what we need to change.

Hopefully you aren't surrounding yourself only with flatterers. At the same time, though, we hope you aren't surrounding yourself only with critics. Neither of those extremes is healthy.

When Solomon mentions the wounds from a friend in Proverbs 27:6, he isn't talking about the perpetual critic. He is pointing out that someone who truly has our back will give us hard truths that hurt at times but are ultimately for our benefit. The constant critic merely wounds to wound, whereas a helpful critique will point out blind spots that we might have missed.

Critics who are only critics limit what we can accomplish. Even Jesus experienced this to a degree in his hometown, where he could do only a few miracles (Mark 6:4–5). He was surrounded by critics, and as difficult as it is to believe, the Bible says he couldn't perform many miracles because of their lack of faith in his ability.

True friends lift us up as well as correct us. As healthy leaders, we need a balance. We need people who will lift us up, because we've seen what's possible for humanity. We've seen it in the negative, but we've also seen it in the positive. When we're surrounded by people who support us and encourage us, we can accomplish much.

At the same time, we need truth even when it doesn't feel good. The goal is to find balance in our friends so we don't operate from a highly inflated ego or do things that get us in trouble. We don't want to walk in delusion of our awesomeness, but neither do we want to walk in perpetual discouragement.

Now, there's one other unhealthy extreme we need to talk about. It's the person who doesn't ever let the people who support them know who they really are. We're talking about the person who hides their true self and never lets anyone get close enough to them to truly support or critique the things they do.

The truth is, we're all guilty of this to a degree. We all hide our true selves a bit. We all have this sense of "If they really knew who I am, they wouldn't want to follow me."

Nobody truly feels like they're enough. (Unless they're the narcissistic, delusional type mentioned above. But if you're reading this, we're willing to bet that isn't you.) We all have this feeling of impostor syndrome, especially the more we accomplish as leaders.

STORY: Jason

I have two friends who are actually impostor syndrome specialists. It's a big component of their careers. Can we just acknowledge that the fact I know two people who specialize in this means impostor syndrome might be a pretty big issue? You can't build a specialist's career on something that rarely happens—much less two specialists' careers.

What does an impostor syndrome expert do in their daily work? These specialists have deep awareness and work in the field of people, psychology, and performance. Practically speaking, they partner as a guide with leaders to identify why those leaders feel they are less than enough even though they have much to offer, and they identify where this feeling might be originating from. Impostor syndrome experts help leaders come up with actionable steps so they can grow while moving forward.

STORY: Jonathan

I work in the church media world—the world of companies that design graphics for churches to use. A while back, I got to see firsthand what true fraud looks like.

A friend of mine went to work for a new company that immediately raised red flags for me. Part of it was the exorbitant salary they offered to pay my friend. I didn't think that was sustainable for any company serving churches, especially knowing their price point. Then I saw these offers repeat with other hires.

In a few months, my friend said that he'd quit his job, citing the fact that he hadn't been paid in three months and never got the benefits he was promised. He relayed to me some of the conversations on the company's Slack channel. The company inflated customer numbers, promised everyone would get paid, and cast a vision for how they were part of something big. I realized it was the classic Silicon Valley–style start-up language. And while I knew the numbers wouldn't work out and this language the company used was largely lies, the language wasn't that different from that of companies that *have* succeeded. It frankly felt like a visionary leader encouraging his team to tough it out through hard times.

This realization made me uncomfortable, because I had to evaluate how many times I've led from a place of vision even when the facts didn't support what I was saying. What made me different? Hopefully strong business sense and a desire to be as honest as possible. But still the discomfort sat with me.

High-level leaders have to lead with vision. They have to believe in their vision and help others believe in it in spite of current circumstances or obstacles that seem insurmountable. And the truth of this can lead them to feel like frauds, so they hide their insecurities from people. They do it on social media. They do it in person. They do it even with those close to them.

But there is a difference between visionary leaders and the fraudsters out there. The fraudsters hide insecurities *and* facts, while visionary leaders share the facts. Healthy leaders even share their doubts. But they also share the opportunity and the vision, trusting that people will get behind them because they see those too.

Don't hide the facts from your people, but also don't hide the true you. You'll accomplish far more with a group of people who truly know you and support you. They can help you know that you're enough.

Surrounding yourself with the right type of people is one of the first steps to knowing you're enough—to leading from a healthy place of confidence.

The Way You Compare Yourself with Others

You may have heard the following quote from the Jesuit priest John Powell: "Comparison is the death of true self-contentment."[1] Comparison, in some ways, will steal our contentment and cause us to feel inferior to others.

At the same time, though, avoiding comparison completely is impossible. We're social creatures. We were made to live in community, and a natural part of community is seeing what others do. We emulate what we admire about others, and we try not to do the things we don't like seeing others do. There's even social pressure that helps shape who we are: we see others being shunned by a group when they behave poorly.

This is human nature, and a certain amount of comparison is healthy. The problem is when comparison turns into competition.

Competition is built on the idea that resources are scarce. There's only one first-place prize. There's only so much money in the world. There's only one top leadership spot. Or we might even believe like Will Ferrell's character in the film *Talladega Nights*: "If you're not first, you're last."[2] Thus, when we see others succeed or see them have something we don't, we feel threatened, because we've approached life from a perspective of competition.

If we approach comparison from a competitive standpoint, we'll always feel inadequate. Or, worse, we'll feel like we're doing well compared to others and be satisfied with our level of leadership, even if there's room for growth and improvement. In 2 Corinthians 10:12, Paul talks about the foolishness of thinking more highly of ourselves than we ought to based on comparison: "When they measure themselves by themselves and compare themselves with themselves, they are not wise."

Healthy comparison comes from a place of teamwork rather than competition. We understand that each person on the team has unique assets they bring to the group. There's even celebration that they have something we don't, because we are all better thanks to our uniqueness. The people on our team sharpen us like iron sharpening iron (Prov. 27:17). We know that two are better than one because they can help us when we fall short (Eccles. 4:9–10). So we aren't threatened when we compare; we're encouraged because we know we can walk together and help each other. There's space for us to be pleased with the part we play on the team.

Paul says it this way in Galatians 6:4–5: "Each of you must examine your own actions. Then you can be proud of your own accomplishments without comparing yourself to others. Assume your own responsibility" (GW).

STORY: Jason

This book is actually a result of this idea of comparison from a place of teamwork. I knew Jonathan from a project he ran a few years back. I'd written some articles for him, but I wouldn't have called him a friend. A few transactional emails don't mean a friendship.

I saw that he'd published a book about church hospitality called *Unwelcome*, so I decided to check it out. When I read it, I thought, *This is the book I wanted to write.*

At first, I had to fight the urge to be jealous. I'd wanted to write a book, but doing so requires a unique set of skills if you don't want to feel like you're banging your head against a wall. And in truth, I had more expertise in the church hospitality space. (From Jonathan: It's true, he does.)

I could have let the jealousy turn into resentment, but instead, I simply sent an email. I didn't even sugarcoat it. I told Jonathan, "This is the book I wanted to write." Then I asked if he'd ever want to work on a project together.

We bounced a few emails back and forth, talking about what might work, and our book *The Come Back Effect* was the result of that exchange. Then we wrote *The Volunteer Effect*. Then *The Volunteer Survival Guide*. Then *The Come Back Culture*. And now this one.

Those books never would have happened, though, if I'd considered Jonathan to be my competition. Instead, I realized we were on the same team and that we each had unique skills to bring to the table. We keep writing books with each other because we value what the other has. We each understand that we're enough for the part we have to offer.

Comparison can be good, but it requires a proper perspective. The good news? We naturally tend to compare ourselves less with people as we get older.[3] Mainly this is because we more often compare ourselves with our own past as we age (which can be its own negative form of comparison).

The better news is that we don't have to wait until we're older to reap the benefits of healthy comparison and stop the negative comparison. The key is teamwork. We contribute to the success of others knowing we're getting to be part of that success. We reach out to help others avoid the mistakes we've made—not from a place of arrogance but from genuine concern for their success.

Having an Accurate Picture of Yourself

Reaping the benefits of healthy comparison, though, requires gaining an accurate picture of who you are and what you bring to the table. This lets you stay in your lane and not feel threatened by someone having something that shouldn't have even been yours in the first place.

STORY: Jonathan

I used to fancy myself a pretty good designer. I worked at a church and did all the design, but when I met my friend Joe Cavazos, I changed my mind about that. His design work put mine to shame.

Then I fancied myself a singer until I met my friend Josh Engler. His voice sounds great, and it seems effortless when he leads worship.

I've noticed that as my network expands, I meet more people with skills that seem to eclipse my own. And in that process, I've had the opportunity to feel inferior or to come to a better understanding of the unique skills and aptitudes I have.

I partnered with Joe to start a company called SundaySocial.tv that makes social media graphics for churches to use. I joined Josh on the worship team and even cowrote a song—"New Start"—for an album he released. I still can't entirely put into words what unique skills I have; I just know that when I partner with skilled friends, we can make some pretty great things.

The more you surround yourself with the right people and the more you team up with people, the more you get a clear picture of yourself. And that's key to understanding that you're enough for the role of leadership you've been given.

Still, the tendency is to focus on what you don't have instead of what you do. Or you focus on your shortcomings instead of your successes. It's a natural human tendency to feel insecure, even if you aren't comparing yourself to others in a competitive way. That eats away at your ability to see yourself accurately.

The thing is, we tend to be gracious toward others and hard on ourselves. When we see a friend fail, it's easy to encourage them: "You learned from that mistake. You've gotten better through it." But when we fail, we say things like, "You're such a failure. You shouldn't have tried that in the first place. Who do you think you are?"

Ouch.

If you want to get an accurate picture of yourself, practice a bit of self-compassion. Tell yourself what you would tell a friend: "You're learning. You're getting better. It's okay that you didn't do everything perfectly." As Christopher Germer and Kristin D. Neff, experts in self-compassion, say, "Self-compassion is simply compassion directed inward."[4]

Have some grace for yourself, knowing that you're a person under development.

Does this sound a little bit like the popular self-love movement? If you're like us, you might want to reject this notion of accepting yourself completely with all your flaws. In fact, Scripture teaches us that we aren't enough. It tells us that we are depraved and no good thing comes from us (Rom. 7:18). At the same time, though, it talks about our magnificence and about us being beautifully designed for a purpose. "For we are God's masterpiece. He has created us anew in Christ Jesus, so we can do the good things he planned for us long ago" (Eph. 2:10 NLT).

The tension there is important. Compare it to the theological truth of justification and sanctification. Justification: we are righteous. Sanctification: we are being made righteous. Both of those are true, and neither by itself shows us the full picture. It's within the tension of justification and sanctification that we can be confident we are saved and are being saved.

This same tension applies to your development as a leader. You are the leader you need to be, but you are also becoming the leader you need to be. It's a tension that feels impossible, but it's the truth.

Can we call that leaderfication? No? Okay. Forget we tried.

Sanctifileadership and justifileadership?

Okay. We'll stop trying. Sorry.

The point is, seeing yourself from this perspective gives you space to grow and to get better. But it also gives you grace for when you make mistakes and fall short.

God designed things this way so that we're constantly relying on him. As soon as we think we've figured things out and put things in their appropriate boxes, we're believing lies and no longer relying on God. We're worshiping a God we created, and that's a recipe for burnout.

Think of the story of Gideon. He was a mess. He was hiding when God called him to fight the battle. Gideon never felt like he was enough. Yet God used him, and God got the glory. (See Judg. 6–7.)

Was Gideon enough? Yes and no. But God said he was enough for what he needed.

What does the Lord say about you? He says you're enough, and you will be enough.

Empower Your Team

Now you're living in that tension of knowing you're the leader you need to be while also becoming the leader you need to be. This is where your team comes in.

You aren't enough for the whole mission. But you're enough for what you need to be. Stop worrying about your shortcomings or your inadequacies and move forward with your team.

As the old saying goes, "Humility isn't thinking less of yourself; it's thinking of yourself less." Trust that you are enough, and empower your team to make up the rest.

One of the imbalances in Western Christianity is the overemphasis on the individual. All of Scripture was written from a "we" perspective, and we don't get an accurate picture of God when we read it solely from an "I" perspective. We are the body of Christ. We are many parts coming together to accomplish the work of God.

Get over individualism when it comes to your leadership. Your team is part of knowing you're enough: you (singular) are enough in the context of your team because you (plural) are enough.

Think of it this way: Individualism is about the contract. Collectivism is about the covenant. Contracts fall apart when one party doesn't accomplish their responsibility. But in covenants, if one party can't accomplish their part of the bargain, another one chips in and does more. When we approach our leadership from a collectivist, covenantal approach, we work together as a team and fill in for each other.

This is what Paul talks about in Ephesians 4:1–2:

> Therefore I, a prisoner for serving the Lord, beg you to lead a life worthy of your calling, for you have been called by God. Always be humble and gentle. Be patient with each other, making allowance for each other's faults because of your love. (NLT)

Do your part, let your team do its part, and let God do his part.

And that ye study to be quiet, and to do your own business, and to work with your own hands, as we commanded you; that ye may walk honestly toward them that are without, and that ye may have lack of nothing. (1 Thess. 4:11–12 KJV)

STORY: Michael Tuszynski, Founder and CEO of Church Media Squad

My first full-time ministry job was directly out of college. I was hired as a combo youth and worship pastor—two full-time jobs on one full-time salary. Quickly I realized that each department I oversaw expected full-time work from the position and I wouldn't be able to do it all.

I'd always had this picture of myself being able to say yes to everything and accomplish it all, almost like I had unlimited capacity. But with this role, I found that wasn't true. I didn't know how to set appropriate expectations for myself, so I always felt like I wasn't adequate for the job.

I burned out. I decided to leave the position and move to a completely different state. Now that I've had some separation from full-time ministry, I'm working on an MDiv degree, and I'd love to be able to be more of a resource to my church from a lay position. But it took me years to feel healthy enough to contribute in a larger capacity to a local congregation.

4 | RELEASE CONTROL

Releasing control generates momentum.

There's a natural tendency, when you're in charge, to try to control as many things as possible. That isn't to say you become an overly controlling leader—manipulating and behaving heavy-handedly with your team—but you have a desire to keep your hands in everything and make sure nothing gets beyond your ability to bring it back into order.

Think of it like a dad teaching his son to drive for the first time. He keeps his hand on the emergency brake to make sure nothing disastrous happens. Many leaders approach their teams that way. They give them just enough responsibility to do their work but not enough that the leader can't pull the brakes and keep them from making a mistake.

More control is healthy when people are brand-new to the process—it can actually set them up for success—but control beyond the learning environment will do one of two things to you and your organization:

1. Control will wear you out as a leader.
2. Control will limit the organization to accomplishing only what you could do.

STORY: Jonathan

Early on in my career, working for my church, I led the tech team. This was the group that ran sound, lights, video, slides, etc. I had a decent team of volunteers, but I had high standards for production quality. I frequently bumped people out of the way to show them how they could do their jobs better. I was far more concerned with having everything perfect than leading a team.

In fact, when we began Sunday evening services—which were low-key, acoustic services meant for only our committed regulars—I decided to run tech for the whole night myself. I did sound, ran slides, and controlled the lights.

Not to brag, but I executed the job flawlessly. Even though this was the service with the lowest stakes, the production quality was probably the best of any of our services.

The problem was, the work began to wear me out—even as a twenty-something with infinite energy.

A member of our pastoral team approached me with that Exodus 18 passage about it not being good to do everything by yourself. I took their admonishment to heart and began relying on my team more. I invited volunteers to be part of the Sunday evening service and even began trusting my team members more in the other services.

As I began to release more control, I had the opportunity to actually leave the tech booth. I found other areas for improvement. I even began noticing first impressions guests must have had at our church and had some things to offer there. I eventually worked myself into roles with bigger influence and more responsibility because I released control to the people I trusted to be on my team.

Your team will never grow or develop as long as you have complete control over it. You'll see this truth in places both big and small, in individual ministries and whole organizations. Control will limit effectiveness and growth.

Having worked with so many churches over the years, we have a theory about church growth. We've noticed there tend to be certain natural limits to the size of a church, depending on the leader.

Some leaders have no problem growing a church to around one thousand people. They blow past all the "church growth barriers" the professional consultants are so quick to list. Yet at the one-thousand-person mark, the church stalls out. Or some pastors get to one hundred. Some to two hundred.

Guests visit the church. Some even stay around. But others seem to leave at the same ratio. The church tends to spend years hovering around that same number.

Our theory isn't that some pastors are more magnetic than others, leading to the differences in the sizes of churches. Instead, it's that each person has a limit to what they can control. Some can control more (like the pastors leading churches of one thousand), while others can control less.

Again, that isn't to say the pastor is a controlling person. Rather, they haven't released control to the people they lead like they need to. They simply can't manage all the things that need to be done as the church grows beyond their capacity, so things slip through the cracks, people stop feeling cared for, or staff members leave for "greener pastures." It's not that the pastor is a bad leader; they've just been stretched beyond their natural capacity to control.

The pastor's biggest asset in the growth season of their church (their ability to bring excellence through their control) can become their liability in the next season (the thing limiting their growth). This same theory applies to smaller teams as well. Control limits the growth and impact of the team to what the leader can accomplish on their own, because everything has to run through them.

Control in leadership looks like this:

- "Check in with me along the way on that project."
- "Let me brainstorm some ideas for you."
- "You don't have to do that part. I'll take care of it for you."
- "While we're at it, what if we tried _____ too?"
- "That's a good idea, but let me take some time to think about it." (Or, similarly, "Let's pray about that before we do anything.")
- The leader constantly modifies the plan.
- The leader repeatedly pops their head in and checks on the progress of a project.

You might be reading this list and thinking, *There's nothing wrong with any of those things.* You're right. But each of those statements puts the ball back in the leader's court and causes people to wait for them to act. The leader is tugging on the emergency brake to make sure the team member doesn't do anything out of their control.

We *should* be checking in with our teams. We *should* be helping them with ideas. We *should* be thinking and praying about action. We *should* be stoking their fire. But those things, for the most part, shouldn't be tugs on the emergency brake. They should be small adjustments to forward progress.

Releasing control means letting momentum happen, even if it can be scary at times. It's letting our teams bring their full energy to their projects.

STORY: Jason

When my wife and I began attending a new church, we loved the senior pastor and felt excited to get involved. But all the volunteer opportunities at the church ran through a separate executive pastor. He was a former pastor of another church and had come in to help the main pastor release some of the control over running the daily operations at the church.

The senior pastor introduced us to the executive pastor, excitedly listing all the things we might be able to help with around the church. I'm sure the senior pastor didn't pick up on this, but I sensed that the executive pastor might have felt a little threatened by the way the other pastor was praising us. He even said something that seemed intended to put me in my place: "What's the name of your company? I've never heard of you."

My wife and I tried to volunteer at the church for five months. I kept attempting to set a meeting with the executive pastor, but he could never commit to a time. Consequently, my wife and I began to realize we might not have a place at that church.

Now, was the issue that the executive pastor felt threatened by me and my wife and didn't want us to get involved in serving? Perhaps, but maybe not. Maybe he just felt overstretched and didn't have the capacity to meet with someone new to bring into the mix.

Regardless, both of those issues come down to control. And the control issue was keeping the teams at that church from growing, even affecting attendance when people who wanted to get involved felt unwelcome.

Weak leaders need control, but the strongest leaders actually welcome people they can't fully control. Great potential can never be controlled, only managed. Control keeps us from getting the best people we can find for our teams.

Some of us have grown up with a style of leadership that says everyone needs to be under control. Others of us just have a hard time releasing control, even though we know that's the best approach.

The reason so many of us have a hard time releasing control is that we usually got our positions of leadership by being good doers. We performed our tasks well, so somebody gave us a leadership position. Naturally, we keep focusing on performing tasks even though what's needed from us has now changed.

The leadership role is a completely different dynamic than the accomplishment of tasks. Leaders aren't doers, but if we haven't made that mental shift, we'll always revert to doing things instead of spending our time leading the people who do the things. And when we don't spend our time leading those people—empowering them to accomplish their tasks—they'll always operate with the barriers of our oversight and feedback. That works as we're starting out, because we can filter everything our teams do through our decisions effectively if we're leading one or three or five (or maybe even twenty) people. But at some point, as the number of people we lead grows, we become a stopping point for our teams. We limit what they can do since everything runs through us.

As leaders, we have to shift our mindset from accomplishing tasks to being okay with our people doing the tasks. That doesn't make us lazy.

This isn't to say we become the commander of an army a whole country away, not feeling the pains and struggles of our team. We can still be in the trenches with people. But instead of being the person fighting the fight, we serve our people. We care for them and find ways to support them in their role. We don't do their tasks for them.

Our contribution to the team isn't diminished; it simply looks different.

Intentionally Controlling?

We're estimating that half of the people reading this right now are thinking, *I can't trust my people enough to release control.*

Many intentionally refuse to release control because they've been burned in the past. But you must. When you choose to release control, you have a higher probability of longevity and long-term influence as a leader.

The problem with control is that it's a mirage. In any organization, large or small, there's a certain amount of chaos. Anytime we get different people with different goals and attitudes and aptitudes together, there's chaotic energy. Control gives us the false impression that the chaos isn't happening. We subconsciously believe, *Chaos isn't chaos when I'm in control of it.* But that's a false perception, and, worse, it makes those we're controlling feel like they're in a chaotic situation. We might not feel the chaos, but our team does. And all the while, we're becoming exhausted trying to keep control from slipping from our grasp.

The only thing you as a high-capacity, healthy leader should be controlling is yourself: your attitude, your reactions, what you say, and what you think. Spend your time controlling those things, and you'll have your hands plenty full.

Let's pause here and ask the following question: Where are you on the control scale? On a scale of 1 to 10—1 being low and 10 being high—how controlling are you in your organization? If you aren't sure, ask others what it's like to be on the other side of your leadership.

How much of your day is spent doing tasks versus leading? For many of you, if you're honest, you'd say 80 percent of your day is spent doing tasks and 20 percent of your day is spent leading others. What if you flipped that? What if 80 percent was spent leading and only 20 percent was spent doing tasks? That's the appropriate ratio.

Your greatest responsibility as a leader is serving your people, not accomplishing tasks. As Jesus said, "Whoever is the greatest should be the servant of the others" (Matt. 23:11 CEV). And true leadership is serving others—not by being busy accomplishing tasks but by empowering others to do the work and serving them along the way.

Imagine what could happen in your leadership if you released control. Imagine leaving on vacation for a month and seeing the organization or team you lead actually grow instead of shrink in your absence. We've seen that happen. It's possible. But it starts with releasing control.

Managing versus Manufacturing Momentum

As you release control in your organization, you'll notice one of two things. Either the momentum picks up or it comes to a crashing halt. Unfortunately, many in leadership who try to release control experience the latter.

As a healthy leader, you should not be the one manufacturing momentum for your organization. Manufacturing momentum looks like

- having to come up with ideas for people instead of them bringing you ideas
- keeping track of schedules—having to set micro deadlines for people so that you see forward progress in new initiatives
- having to do research for people
- tracking down basic resources that people should already have access to in order to accomplish their jobs

- constantly asking your team, "Why is this next step not done?"

Healthy leadership is about managing momentum; otherwise you're going to grow exhausted. Managing momentum looks like

- choosing from ideas that team members bring
- trusting people will meet deadlines and update you along the way as they make forward progress
- trusting the research others have done and trusting them to make the right decision with the facts they've gathered
- helping people with things only you can do, knowing they've used all the resources available to them to get as far in the project as they can on their own

If you're the one having to create the forward motion, one of two things is going on: either you've limited your team so much that they've settled into being pushed, or you have the wrong person on your team.

They've Settled into Being Pushed

Many leaders who seek to release control and create momentum that isn't dependent on them deal with team members who have to be pushed. People are used to being limited. They're used to having their best efforts toward forward progress slowed down by having to run everything by their leader. They've lost motivation.

Assume this is the case before you assume you have the wrong person on your team. In general, especially in a ministry context, people want to accomplish great things. They want to bring their ideas to the table and follow through on them. If they've settled into being pushed, it's time to remotivate them.

Motivation comes from the answers to these two questions:

1. *How likely am I to succeed if I try?* If you haven't given your team resources to succeed, then they won't even try. Or, worse, if they feel like someone will throw a kink into their plan, they'll hesitate to bring new ideas to the table. If this has happened continually in the past, it'll take time to regain trust.

2. *How much will I get out of this when I do try?* People want to know what's in it for them. Even the most altruistic person wants to get something for their efforts. Now, that doesn't necessarily mean money. In truth, money tends not to motivate people in the long run. Instead, things like achievement, recognition, fulfilling work, more responsibility, and chances for advancement will motivate them. Do your team members see opportunity for one of those things if they take the risk and try something new?

You'll know you have a motivated team when you see them putting discretionary effort into the job. Discretionary effort is time and energy that you can't ask for. It's when team members step out of their job description and give you more because they're motivated to do so.

For instance, picture needing someone to run a food distribution outreach on a Saturday—a day when most of your team rests in preparation for Sunday. A motivated worship leader might volunteer. This task doesn't fall into the typical job description of a worship leader (though caring for those less fortunate in the name of Jesus is pure worship). But because that person is motivated, they're willing to donate their discretionary time and energy to accomplish the goal. They don't do so because they're afraid they'll get fired or displease their pastor if they don't volunteer. Rather, they believe they'll get something out of it.

Churches are notorious for placing unspoken expectations on "discretionary effort." Some expect their employees to volunteer on weekends or work forty hours during the week while also attending all three church services on the weekend. If something is an expectation, it isn't discretionary effort. And expecting something that should be discretionary is a recipe for *their* burnout.

You Have the Wrong Person on Your Team

However, sometimes motivation isn't the issue. Sometimes you just have the wrong person on your team. If you've coached them, worked at establishing trust, and supplied resources and incentives for their success, and they still aren't motivated, they might just be the wrong person for the role on your team.

That isn't to say everyone needs to be a momentum machine in your organization. Every organization needs steady administrators who aren't pushing the envelope and trying new things every time. They're the ones who value stability and accuracy. These people want to know exactly what their role is and want to accomplish only that. But if they are all you have on your team, you'll constantly feel like you're the one creating momentum.

STORY: Jonathan

As an action-oriented leader, I tend to value people who are action-oriented as well. But I've learned I need some people in my organization who are steady-minded. They're the people who require very little maintenance because they just do the same thing month after month. I check in each month to make sure they have what they need, but otherwise they don't need much input from me.

At the same time, even with my action-oriented hires, I tend to require people who don't need too much control from me. We've had interns or other hires who constantly looked for feedback or waited for me to tell them exactly what they needed to do, and it didn't work out. I've found that the key to my survival as a business leader—one who runs multiple businesses as well as writes books like this one—is to have people who know how to prioritize and make decisions, understanding that I hired them for a reason. This has allowed SundaySocial.tv to grow to 4,500 paying subscribers (as of the writing of this book), with only two part-time founders.

When it comes to finding people who will create momentum that you get to manage, you're looking for those who show steady progress, not frenetic energy, in their lives. They should seem more like a train and less like a meadow of fireflies with random bursts of energy and no focus. Ideally, you can just be the train tracks to keep them headed in the right direction.

Look for people who are showing momentum in their lives. Is their marriage improving? Are they working on a side hustle? Are they involved with their children's school? People who bring momentum to your organization generally have momentum in other areas of their lives. (Side note: If they're working hard on a side hustle and not bringing momentum to your organization, it's again an issue of motivation, not necessarily them being the wrong person for the job.)

When you know you have the right people in the right roles, guide them, reward them, and empower them. When people feel trusted and supported, they'll give you their best work, which in turn encourages you to guide, reward, and empower them more. This becomes a cycle of momentum, and that's a powerful thing that will help you thrive in your leadership.

Our friend Daniel Villarreal, a pastor in San Antonio, Texas, saw the power of this in his church. Bouncing back and forth between hospital wings as he cared for his wife and newborn baby, he had no energy or time to devote to the church. But because he had built an organization filled with trust and momentum and had learned to let go of control, when he returned to his role at the church, the church had actually grown.

This is the power of having an organization whose momentum you manage instead of manufacture. It can keep thriving even when you need a break for a season.

What If You Have the Wrong Person in the Role?

If, after you've coached someone, you find out they're still the wrong person for the role—they're someone you can't release control to— you have three options:

1. Remove them.
2. Reposition them.
3. Demote them.

Do you feel uncomfortable reading that? Even people in businesses feel weird about those options. Churches especially feel like these are dirty words, because our job, first and foremost, is to care for people, right?

Well, one of the most loving things you can do for people is to put them in a role where they'll thrive. Team members know when they aren't excelling. It can be frustrating for people to feel like they aren't succeeding, and that's a recipe for their own burnout. Why not help yourself and help them thrive by finding the right role for them?

Consider this story. We have a friend who works for a church. He's a graphic designer, and he's really good at graphic design. He sat down with us recently, though, to tell us he was growing dissatisfied at his church. He felt like it might be time to quit. So we asked him about his role.

Recently, his team had noticed how good he was at his job, and they promoted him to a leadership role. They wanted him to lead other graphic designers.

He took that role, then found himself so busy managing other designers that he wasn't able to design—the thing he loves doing. He felt like he was ineffective as a designer *and* as a leader, and he was losing motivation.

We made a bold suggestion to him. "What if you ask to be demoted?"

He didn't know how to respond to that at first. It felt contrary to everything he'd been taught by our culture—that leadership is the greatest goal for anyone in ministry.

But we pressed the issue. "You're a designer. You're excellent at design. And when that was exclusively what you were doing, you loved your role at the church. You'd never thought of leaving before now."

He considered that and realized it was true.

As a culture, we're trained to believe that success equals more and better. Better pay. Better title. More responsibility. We're constantly reaching for more, thinking it will lead us to happiness and fulfillment.

The problem is, that's not true. Sometimes the most freeing thing you can do is choose the job with less pay, less stress, and more margin.

As a church culture, similarly, we have this mentality that everyone ultimately needs to become a leader. While everyone should seek to influence and encourage people as believers, some highly skilled roles shouldn't be interrupted by leadership responsibilities. If someone's a highly skilled designer, let them design.

So what happens when there's someone you can't release control to? Do you fire them? Do you find another role more suited to their skills? Or do you demote them back to their area of success? It'll be different for each situation, and communication will be the key to finding the right solution.

One of the most freeing things you can do as a leader is have the right people in the right roles in your organization and be able to release control to them.

Imagine spending the majority of your day encouraging people instead of scrambling to manage tasks. Imagine having emotional energy to develop new ideas. Imagine having a motivated team that, when you present those ideas, gets excited to be part of them.

When you release control to your team in a healthy way, this becomes possible.

STORY: Justin Trapp, CEO of Ministry Pass

One of the healthiest things I experienced in ministry was when I began a new job at Westover Hills Church in San Antonio, Texas. About ten months into my role there, Jim Rion called me into his office and let me go. It wasn't for anything I had done. Instead, it had become apparent that I wasn't ready for the role I was filling in the season of intense growth the church was experiencing.

The reason I say this is healthy is because he believed he could get me ready, but it would be a difficult two-year journey and he didn't want to put me through that. He said he was okay with me not liking him, but he refused to be responsible for me burning out in ministry right out of the gate.

I have always respected him and that decision. The older I get, the more I appreciate the care he showed to me through that difficult decision and conversation.

5 | HUMBLE YOURSELF

Humility in leadership is strength.

Humility is one of those difficult concepts in Christianity. You know the classic story of the church deacon who was given a blue ribbon for being the most humble in the church. The problem was, they had to take it away from him for wearing it.

Pastors love to tell that story, but the truth is, we hate to hear it. It misses the point about what humility really is. If you're truly humble, you can say you're humble. Jesus did. When he said, "Let me teach you, because I am humble" (Matt. 11:29 NLT), he wasn't bragging. He was acknowledging the truth of the situation.

Jesus was bold in his humility. For him, humility wasn't weakly pretending that he didn't have the most important things in the world to teach his disciples.

Humility isn't denying the truth; it's denying yourself. Humility is revolving yourself around others instead of having them all revolve around you.

It's important to accurately understand humility because it can be difficult in high-functioning leadership. On one end of the spectrum you have leaders who are bashful about leading for fear of appearing prideful, and on the other you have narcissistic leaders who make the whole organization about themselves. If you're the former, you probably aren't getting much done. If you're the latter, there's a real problem and a huge potential for burnout. (Not to mention moral failures.)

It's easy for narcissism to enter the equation of leadership. If you're an effective leader, you've probably built an effective organization that's genuinely helping people. Lives are changing, and your influence as a leader is helping to make that happen. You're doing the work of God! Consequently, the organization can be placed on a pedestal as something that needs to be protected and served at all costs. Its goals become the only goals that matter.

And there's where it gets sticky. Who's leading the organization? You are. So is it the organization's goals that get all the attention, or is it yours? Do its members revolve around you, or do they revolve around the organization?

As much as we want to make the focus God's vision or the collective community of those involved in the organization, the leader gets a lot of the focus of the energy of those involved. The leader is the one deciphering God's goal for the organization. Add to that the tendency of people to express their delight with how much the organization has impacted their lives and the leader's role in that, and a leader can very easily become Narcissus, the man in Greek mythology who fell so in love with his reflection that he couldn't look away.

When this happens, everything and everyone become tools for the "organization"—which is largely the leader—to use. Everyone serves at the pleasure of the king. And no matter how meek a leader might appear, if they see the members of their organization this way, they're filled with pride, and it will lead to devastating burnout.

What's the solution to this? Should the leader take a sabbatical until they can regain proper perspective on their role in the vision for the organization? Maybe. That might be something they need to do.

But there's another way. And it's modeled in how Jesus treated his disciples.

If ever there was a leader who could develop narcissistic tendencies, it would be Jesus. He performed miracles that baffled the world. He had thousands following him, even into situations where there was no food available. People went to their death for Jesus. He was about to change the way humans and God related to each other. History hinged on his life and death.

Yet Jesus was humble. How?

He always served his disciples in a greater way than they served him. Yes, they did the tasks Jesus told them to do. Yes, they served Jesus greatly. But Jesus always humbled himself to a position of a servant for them. He showed that every part of the organization—his ministry—mattered.

- *The leader mattered.* Jesus frequently went away to pray by himself to get rest and to refuel with his Father.
- *The people being blessed by his ministry mattered.* He kept teaching and healing.
- *The team members working alongside him mattered.* He knelt to wash their feet. He gave his all for them.

Humbling yourself in a way that leads to long-term, high-capacity leadership is choosing to revolve your life around others, not having them revolve around you. It's following Paul's advice in Philippians 2:4—"not looking to your own interests but each of you to the interests of the others."

Humbling yourself means refusing to sacrifice individuals on the altar of the organizational vision. It means directing, correcting, firing, and promoting from a place of love and genuine interest in the value of others, not seeing them just as tools of the organization.

STORY: Jason

One boss I worked for had a habit of sacrificing individuals on the altar of the organization.

Now, I have a great work ethic. I work a lot. And at the time, I was already working seventy-plus-hour weeks. But my boss told me, "If you leave at 5:00 p.m. every day, you aren't busy enough." He believed the organization was the ultimate good and that we owed it all of our time and energy.

I had to move into a house one street over from the church just so I could still see my family and fulfill the demands that this leader made on my time. He was willing to sacrifice me and my family for the sake of the church.

We served the church, but ultimately that meant we served him. He did not serve us.

Championing Your Team Members' Dreams

People in your organization have their own God-given dreams for their lives. Maybe they want a marriage that's stronger than the one their parents had. Maybe they have a goal of serving as a missionary for a few years overseas. Or maybe they have a talent that isn't getting an outlet.

Many leaders who have allowed narcissism to enter their leadership have the unfortunate perspective that people shouldn't have dreams separate from the organization. These leaders see side hustles or time spent away from the organization as disloyalty. That's toxic leadership, and it's eventually headed for a tragic explosion.

If you're reading this book—a book about healthy, long-term leadership—there's a good chance that type of leader isn't you. But the question is, Do you know the dreams of your team members?

STORY: Jason

Throughout my twenty-five years of working in the church, I've worked for some amazing leaders who have invested in me as a leader in their organization. They've given me a chance to develop new skills and truly excel in my leadership.

The best boss I ever had was a man named Chris Green. He was the first person to ask me about my dreams beyond the confines of our organization. Not only that, but he proactively asked me what was standing in the way of achieving those dreams. He encouraged me to take action on them.

After the fifth time of him following up with me on the progress of my dreams, I said, "Wow, you really *are* interested!" It surprised me.

The interesting thing about him doing this was that it made me better at my job. It made me better at a lot of things in life. And chasing my dreams outside the organization didn't hurt my productivity within it.

Could you jot down the major members of your team right now and list the dreams they have? If not, we encourage you to ask them. If you're grabbing coffee before a meeting, just say to a team member, "I've always wondered—what would you like your life to look like in five years?" Or, "What's something you've always wanted to accomplish?"

Depending on your team members' previous experience in the church world, they might be wary of answering this truthfully. After all, there's a chance they've worked with narcissistic leaders who discouraged pursuits beyond the confines of the organization. But if you keep asking and checking in, you'll eventually get their true response. It's hard for people to hide their dreams for too long.

Now that you know their dreams, are you helping them achieve them? There are some simple ways you can do this as a leader:

- Encourage them to try something.
- Ask questions so you understand their dreams better.
- Help them clarify what might seem a bit foggy in their head.
- Supply them with personal connections, books, articles, videos, etc.
- Give them time off for their dreams.

After reading this list, you might be thinking, *This is great, Jason and Jonathan. But what's in it for me if I help them accomplish their dreams? This will take more work from me.*

We don't judge you for asking that. If you already feel over-stretched with your own dream, how can you possibly help others with theirs? How can this possibly lead to healthy, long-term leadership for you?

It comes down to the principle of sowing and reaping. What you plant, you harvest. And that principle in Scripture doesn't apply just to money. It applies to anything we can invest in, which includes the dreams of others.

Proverbs 11:24–25 says, "The world of the generous gets larger and larger; the world of the stingy gets smaller and smaller. The one who blesses others is abundantly blessed; those who help others are helped" (MSG).

That picture of your world getting larger is powerful, especially if you've ever felt trapped by your role in leadership. If you've ever felt stuck, this proverb gives the solution. Invest in others. Bless others. Help others with their dreams.

We get life when we give life. We get help with our visions when we give help to others' visions. It's a principle of the universe God set into motion, and it works whether you're a believer or not.

Not only that, but there's something energizing about playing a role in someone else's story. It's like the proud mom who sees her daughter begin a family of her own. She has invested so much into her daughter's life, and getting to see that repeated with the next generation is energizing. Even though she's done with the baby stage, she's excited to chip in and help take care of the baby. Seeing her daughter thrive makes her thrive.

One of the most energizing things we've ever done as leaders is to call out the talents of our team members and help them develop those talents.

Consider the young people on your team especially. One of the most valuable things you can offer them as a leader and mentor is helping them see themselves. When you notice they're good at something, call it out. Point out how their skill might be used in other ways. Young people rarely get that. Usually authorities in their lives are busy correcting them. Consequently, they'll go to the first person who reaches out to them on LinkedIn and shows them an opportunity they think is tailor-made for them.

So if for no other reason than the selfish one of not losing your people, invest in the talents and dreams of your team members.

STORY: Jason

One time after a meeting, one of my coworkers came in to talk to me. She bragged on a volunteer of hers, Sam, who was downstairs doing things to help out.

I'm always on the lookout for young leaders who have potential, so I decided to engage Sam to see if he really was everything I'd just been told.

Sam explains it like this: "It was so weird. Out of nowhere, Jason appears and begins talking to me. He's asking me questions. And in a few minutes, he offers me an internship."

That internship became a part-time job. Then Sam left to go to another part of the organization for a full-time role. I kept investing in him. Then he switched to another campus. To this day, I still invest in him, because I saw his potential and wanted to be part of his trajectory.

Opportunities for Growth

Along with championing your team members' dreams outside the organization, you should be providing opportunities for growth within it as well.

Integrate the talents and aptitudes you're noticing in your team members into the organization, and look for new roles that can allow those talents to shine. Then proactively move people into those roles. You might even set a recurring item on your to-do list: spending an hour evaluating the people on your team and looking for ways you can grow them in the organization.

STORY: Jason

When I first started at North Point Ministries years ago, I took a break from speaking and writing for a year to demonstrate to my new bosses and to myself that I was truly invested in the organization. It was just a personal goal I set for myself.

When that year was over, I approached my boss and asked about beginning to speak and write again. He encouraged me with, "Absolutely. Do it."

His reasoning was that speaking and writing would help make me better. When you talk about and teach something, it tends to sharpen your knowledge. He knew it would make me better because I could also see and experience what was happening at the other organizations where I spoke.

80

Andy Stanley had that same philosophy as I began working more directly with him.

Obviously I still had to get my day job done. But outside gigs didn't threaten my leadership because my bosses knew it was valuable to let my dreams flourish.

One of the reasons people so often share their gifts and talents outside the church is that there's no outlet for them in the church. This is why so many side hustles start. This is why people build speaking or writing platforms. They have an itch that isn't getting scratched in the organization.

Now, it's important to remember that having interests and building things outside the organization isn't bad. Those will always happen. But it's important to understand why. Are they happening because people aren't getting opportunities within the ministry or simply because they have a dream for something bigger? The former is a sad reality many organizations deal with; the latter is perfectly normal.

What happens in a lot of ministries is that a select few get all the growth opportunities. Usually they're the leader's favorites— the people who have been there from the beginning or who most reflect the leader's own personality. Sometimes they're the people the leader can control most easily.

Evaluate your ministry. Who's growing right now? Who's getting put into new roles? Is it time to revisit chapter 4 ("Release Control") and grow some people in your organization who might not be your "favorites"?

The by-product of doing this is that you get to do more of the things that energize you. When you give away more of your leadership responsibilities to people in your organization, you get emotional and physical energy back.

Not only that, but as people grow in your organization, their excitement pulls you along. You get to drift off some of their momentum.

Grace-Filled Gratitude

Acknowledging team members who need to grow within the organization requires the humility of gratitude. Gratitude sees other people's contributions and values them. And a proper position of gratitude toward your people helps keep you humble.

Now, you're in ministry. You know that gratitude is important. But what we're talking about is the next phase of it: grace-filled gratitude.

STORY: Jonathan

I have a small, shared office in my coworking space. A few Realtors share the office with me, so we frequently listen in on each other's conversations and chime in. Let me tell you, I know way more about the San Antonio housing market than I should.

One day I was telling one of my friends in the office that my wife had encouraged me to take a solo trip to Universal Studios. I'm a 7 on the Enneagram scale, so I'm all about fun, fun, fun.

One of the other Realtors in the office chimed in. "Your wife told you to go to Universal Studios by yourself? And leave her alone with your baby?"

"Yep."

"But, like, you know she's going to be texting you sarcastic things about how you're having fun without her and she's miserable at home with the baby."

"No, she really won't. She legitimately wants me to go and have a good time."

In that moment, I turned into the marriage guru in my coworking space.

The disbelief and questions went flying. They finally verbalized the question "How did you do it?" So I answered.

When my wife needed to go to Miami to spend time with her cousin who was in the hospital, I willingly volunteered to take care of our baby while she was gone for three days. Then, while she was there, I sent her smiling pictures of the baby, reinforcing how well he was doing.

The natural tendency would be to show her that he was crying. That he pooped through his diaper. That he had a fever one night. But I chose not to do that (and in general, that's how we go about it when we're at home alone with the baby), and her gratitude spilled out into suggesting I take a trip.

The Realtors were in awe of my wisdom (as they should have been).

But wouldn't you know, I ruined the whole experience two hours before writing this story. I reminded my wife that my trip to Universal Studios was payback for watching our baby while she was in Miami.

Can you guess what happened? All the gratitude left. I basically told her that she owed me, and it has taken a few hours to regain the gratitude in our relationship.

Grace-filled gratitude is a mixture of two things: being thankful for someone doing something for you, and avoiding the concept that someone owes you something.

Expectations can hurt relationships. When someone owes you something based on an expectation or something you think you earned, it's hard to be grateful for it. And when you're a leader (especially if you sign paychecks), it can be really tempting to think people owe you something as they work for you.

- They owe you because they signed up to volunteer.
- They owe you because you trusted them with a unique opportunity.

- They owe you because you work ten times harder than they do.
- They owe you because you're paying them.

When you have the concept that people owe you, it removes humility from the mix, because it puts you on a pedestal. It sets you up as a lofty being to be served. Worse than that, it adds pressure to you, because you get the faulty notion that everything ultimately falls on your shoulders. If people owe you, that means you paid the great price of sacrifice that made their work an equitable trade.

But gratitude—grace-filled gratitude—has the opposite effect. It puts you in a humble position and takes the pressure off you as a leader.

And here's the fun thing about grace-filled gratitude. It becomes a cycle. Gratitude creates more gratitude. So as you have a grateful attitude toward your team members, they begin to have a grateful attitude toward you. They work harder, giving you another reason to be grateful. You reward their hard work, which gives them even more reason to be grateful.

If this hasn't been the norm for your leadership, it might be hard to feel genuine, grace-filled gratitude toward your team. Fortunately, there are some things you can be grateful for right now to get the cycle started.

- Your team member showed up to work. (Maybe not on time, but they still showed up.)
- They aren't flirting with moral failure, potentially creating a massive mess for you to clean up.
- They aren't trash-talking you and trying to usurp your authority. (Or at least they have the decency to do so behind your back.)

This list might seem a bit ridiculous because it feels like you're setting the bar at the bare minimum, but you still have reason to celebrate these things. Unfortunately, this bare minimum isn't the reality a lot of times, even in the church world. We've all seen power struggles, lazy people, moral failures . . . They're far too common.

In Philippians 2:15, after a lengthy passage about being humble and having gratitude in the way you approach those around you, Paul offers a great promise. He says that if you keep humble and stay grateful, "you will shine among them like stars in the sky." You'll be able to burn bright.

Make Them Look Good

Finally, one great way you can humble yourself as a leader is to make your team members look good.

We love to tell employees to make their bosses look good; it's the key to promotions and pay raises. But did you know it's just as important for bosses to make their employees look good? There are obvious benefits like motivation and morale, but the greatest benefit will be your longevity in leadership.

Making your team members look good starts with a few key questions:

- Do you reward them for trying, even if they failed?
- Do you set them up for success?
- Do you give them a platform for their gifts?
- Do you provide safe environments to learn?
- Do you reinforce that they're excelling at their jobs?

Your team members should never wonder if you think they're doing a good job. If they aren't, tell them and give them steps to improve. If they are, make sure everyone knows.

Don't make your team members brag about their own accomplishments. You should be the one bragging on them first. (And not in a way that makes you look good for hiring them.)

A good way to look at it is this: Spend more time being impressed than impressing. Be genuinely impressed with your team members, and it'll be easy to make them look good. Too often we spend all our efforts making sure we look good, but that comes from a position of insecurity.

That sense of being impressed with others is one of the things that makes Jimmy Fallon such a likable late-night host. When he listens to the stories of his guests, he makes them feel like their story is the funniest thing he's ever heard. And he does it genuinely. It doesn't matter if he's just met the guest. It doesn't matter if they've been his friend for decades. It doesn't matter if they're a new star who barely made the guest list or the president of the United States. He acknowledges the gift they gave him by being on his show. And he does it with genuine interest. You can hear it in his words, but you can also see it in his body language. Jimmy Fallon doesn't spend his time making sure people like him; he spends his time making his guests the stars.

Like Mr. Fallon, some people seem to have this natural ability to find everyone genuinely interesting. Others have to develop the talent.

Do you find yourself in the second group? Here's a hack that can help you start finding others interesting. Ask yourself these questions when you talk to someone:

- What do they know that I don't?
- What perspective do they have that I don't?
- What have they overcome that I can learn from?

86

The truth is, everyone has something to offer you. And it's not just in connections and other favors they can do for you in the future. Even people who will never be able to do a single thing for you have value to you because you can learn from them. Sometimes they don't even know what's of value inside them, but you can make it your task to tease it out and help them see it too. You just have to truly believe that everyone has something of value to reveal.

Jesus was in the habit of seeing value in those society discarded. He saw value in children. In the sick. In the Samaritans. In the disabled.

He spent time with people. He walked among them. He marveled at their faith. He answered questions. He touched and healed.

Paul talks about Jesus in Philippians 2, which we've already referenced a couple times in this chapter, and shows how Jesus approached valuing others. In verses 3–8, Paul tells us how to be humble:

Do nothing out of selfish ambition or vain conceit. Rather, in humility value others above yourselves, not looking to your own interests but each of you to the interests of the others.

In your relationships with one another, have the same mindset as Christ Jesus:

Who, being in very nature God,
did not consider equality with God something to be used
to his own advantage;
rather, he made himself nothing
by taking the very nature of a servant,
being made in human likeness.
And being found in appearance as a man,
he humbled himself
by becoming obedient to death—
even death on a cross!

Following that, Paul gives us the results of Jesus's humility in verse 9: "Therefore God exalted him to the highest place."

God exalted Jesus for his humility, and that promise of exaltation is made to us as well. When we adopt the same attitude of humility and service that Jesus had, God lifts us up. We don't have to worry about showing others how great we are; we can trust God to take care of what needs to happen on our behalf. Our job is just to humble ourselves.

STORY: Rommel Manio, Campus Experience Pastor at Saddleback Church, Lake Forest, California

I believe the key to my longevity in ministry has been to delegate. I strategically delegate opportunities for people to lead and learn. I bring people in, partner with them, then release them to do great work.

I want to champion what's inside my team members. After all, I feel like that is what the Holy Spirit does inside of us. He brings to life what is in us. He helps us figure out where we can minister. If I can be part of that for my team members, I want to be.

The way I approach championing people is to listen to their goals, then help them with a strategic plan. I ask them the following questions: What can you control? What will take input from others? What will take more time? Then I help them say yes to things that lead them toward their goals.

6 | ESTABLISH AND OPERATE FROM VALUES

Wise decisions come from priorities in order.

This world wants us to compromise our values. Culture wants us to choose finances over family. Performance over peace. Influence over impact. The world wants us to chase things that lead, long term, to dissatisfaction and exhaustion.

Unless we—especially as leaders—keep laser-focused on the values that will lead to life, we're doomed to such a future. However, when we stay on the path that leads to life, focused on God-given values, we can experience longevity in leadership.

We're all tempted to veer off that path, though. We've all found ourselves straying from appropriate values. There are a few things that cause us to do that:

- Losing focus on what truly matters. We begin chasing things like money, power, security—things that were meant to be tools used by God, not goals in and of themselves.

- A perceived promise of peace, happiness, and true contentment.
- Seeking something to fill a hole in our souls.
- Our ego. We find our intentions shifting from good to bad, and the truth is, it's hard to discern our true motives. Even those of us with the best motives find ourselves with bad ones at times. Our motives drift.
- The fact that bad priorities are often easier to measure than good ones. For instance, there isn't an app that tells us how well our relationships are going. We can't see a 10 percent increase from previous months. Our bank account app, on the other hand . . .

STORY: Jason

One of my top six values is family. (See appendix B for a chart of those values.) I do my best to balance all six, but what I've often seen is that one value easily takes over the others if I'm not careful. There's been a time when one of my values has looked at the others and said, "I'm more important than you."

My passion for work, ministry, and building something has become greater than my family at times. I've taken on more than I should, said yes to too much, and found myself taken away from my family.

The devious thing about this, though, is that I began to make more money, which tempted me to do it even more. I let money, which previously I'd intended to be used to take care of my family, actually eclipse my family.

When I was rewarded for my misaligned values, I got a taste of what felt like satisfaction to me. I wanted more. Then before long, I didn't realize I was far down the road, chasing something that ultimately wouldn't fulfill me. It was like a drug: it gave instant pleasure but faded fast. That eventually led to exhaustion.

I've had to learn how to integrate my different values so they can all play well on the same field. I don't always get it right, but more awareness of the fact that I can so easily fall into this trap has helped me keep focused on my values.

Especially in roles of leadership, it's far too easy to gain your personal value from the work you do. In fact, when introducing yourself, there's a good chance you define yourself based on your profession. "I'm a pastor." "I'm a worship leader." "I'm a minister of _____."

Instead of you saying "I work as a pastor," the role becomes an identity for you. But you're more than your job. And properly aligned values will help you understand that and operate from a place of health.

You see, your values are a sort of road taking you to an eventual destination. If you have the wrong values, you'll find yourself on the wrong road going to the wrong destination in your future. And you can't just accidentally get back on the right road if you're on the wrong one. Neither can you hope your way onto the right road. No, you have to exit the wrong road and find your way back onto the right one.

We believe you can do that; it just requires understanding where you are and recognizing where you want to be, then moving toward that goal.

So take a moment to ask yourself this question: "Do I have my priorities out of order?"

It's time to evaluate things you're reaching for that ultimately don't fall in line with God's plan for you. Evaluate which priorities are out of line. Discover what great things you're sacrificing for something that's only good.

Some of the bad priorities people tend to chase are

- perfection
- success or prestige
- money
- pleasure
- image
- acceptance
- winning
- being right
- security
- being in charge
- peace at the expense of what's right
- growth for the sake of growth

Do you resonate with anything on this list?

Some of those priorities are obviously bad, but some might make you scratch your head. Why did we include those?

Not every priority on the list is inherently bad, but those things aren't meant to be priorities. For instance, security is a good thing. But when it becomes the top priority in our lives, we're resisting the call of God to step away from security and rely on him. The same is true for money. For pleasure. For being in charge.

Priorities are the things we set as authorities in our lives, and we have to be careful what they tell us to do. Bad priorities will exhaust us. They'll set us up to lose things that truly matter in life.

Good priorities, on the other hand, are things like

- excellence
- making an eternal difference
- empathy for others

- doing what's right
- including others
- letting truth win out
- obeying God's call
- loyalty and integrity
- peace as much as it depends on us
- making wise decisions

Good priorities can bring peace to our lives. They can leave us with enough energy to get things done. But even more than that, good priorities, when acted on, can often lead us to things on the previous list—the things that make for bad priorities. For instance, Proverbs is filled with lessons that doing what's right, letting truth win out, and obeying God can lead to riches, long life, and influence.

Matthew 6:33 says, "But seek first the kingdom of God and his righteousness, and all these things will be added to you" (ESV). When we put the right things first, the other things come along.

STORY: Jonathan

My friend runs a community for creative church leaders. One day I was talking to him, and I could tell he was discouraged. He was talking about either selling the community or just shutting it down entirely.

I asked some probing questions. I actually considered buying access to the community for one of the projects I run. But as we got deep into the problem, we realized it was just a misalignment of priorities. One of the advertisers that helped support the community was making my friend compromise the values he had for what he wanted to build. They were paying a lot of money so they could promote their products in more aggressive ways, but it was draining the energy from my friend. He'd needed the money to be able to support the mission of his organization, but he'd had to compromise his priorities to get there.

As we talked it out, he realized it was time to cut ties with the advertiser. (Fortunately, I was willing to take over their spot.) And at the end of the conversation, he'd regained an excitement for the community he'd built. He realigned his values and began launching new, exciting parts to the community that also led to increased income in other areas.

Getting our priorities in order is sometimes as simple as making one big change, but sometimes it requires many smaller changes.

We've all heard the adage "Show me your bank account and calendar, and I'll show you your priorities." But our bank accounts and calendars don't just reflect our priorities; they can actually change our priorities.

The Scripture "Where your treasure is, there your heart will be also" (Matt. 6:21) isn't just a message about showing us our priorities. It can also become a promise of hope for us. Where we put our treasure, our hearts tend to follow. The same is true of our tasks. The tasks we set for ourselves can actually help us align our priorities.

Look at the following:

- calendar items
- budget percentages
- emails you send
- weekly meetings
- books on your shelf
- people who have access to you

Do those reflect the priorities and values you want to establish in your life? If not, it's time to start changing some tasks. Add more calendar items that reinforce the values you want to have. Remove those that don't. Start spending more money in line with the priorities you want to have in your life. Eliminate other expenses. Start scheduling meetings that accomplish the things that truly matter and cut the meetings that don't.

STORY: Jonathan

I have a friend who's a freelance designer. He's also building a platform on social media, helping other freelancers through podcasts and encouraging posts. He invited me to join him on one podcast, and we agreed on a time.

A day later, he texted me, "I'm so sorry. This is totally dumb, but I have to reschedule our podcast recording. Once a year, when baseball season starts, my wife and I go to the park and just walk around all day. It's really dumb, but it's really important to us. I'm so sorry."

I texted back, "You should do stuff like this more often than once a year. I'm fine to reschedule."

One of the benefits of being self-employed is you can do things like that. You can do "dumb things" that reinforce your values. One of my friend's priorities is his wife, so I wanted to encourage him to change his task items to reinforce time with her.

It never gets easier to get your priorities in order. Life will always try to get them out of whack, so it's important to take the opportunities you're presented with to actually follow your values.

Now, how do you determine your values? True values aren't something you can just make up. There's a good chance God has already hardwired your values into you. Sometimes, though, you have to dig into them to truly understand them.

STORY: Jonathan

I was working with a church that was concerned with why they weren't larger than they were. Their pastor had a national platform, yet their attendance was only five hundred people at most. While driving me to their church, one of the team members asked my perspective on it.

I told him all the usual things about church growth. They were already doing them.

In truth, I had no idea what to say to him. But as we spoke more, it became evident what was going on.

Their pastor (this staff member's dad) valued a prison ministry they ran. Not only did they minister to people in the prisons, but they also discipled and walked with them when they got out of prison.

My new friend told me about how he'd been up at 2:00 a.m. helping one of their church members dispose of some drugs that he'd been tempted to use. They sat for about four hours as my friend discipled and encouraged him.

"That right there is the reason your church isn't growing," I told him.

"Huh?"

"Well, you're busy ministering to people who need a lot of time and attention, and there are only so many people you can reach doing that. Your time is spent with emergencies, and the people who largely have their lives together don't feel cared for in your church. So they don't stick around."

He was discouraged, but I spoke further.

"You know, church growth isn't the only metric of success. If your pastor (and obviously you, by the looks of it) values discipling people who need this much attention, you should keep doing it. That obviously is a priority for you, and it's a really good priority. Keep doing that and don't worry so much about attendance numbers. You're accomplishing the purposes that align with your true values. You should be proud."

Your values won't be the same as other people's. Your priorities won't be the same. But if you're acting in accordance with the values and priorities God has for you, you can be sure you're doing the right thing. God loves to strengthen us and encourage us as we move toward his calling.

Work-Arounds

For goal-oriented people, there's a huge temptation to be short-term focused. They create work-arounds to get things done.

If you've been successful as a leader, there's a good chance you've become really good at work-arounds. Creative leaders excel at them, which is part of why they become leaders in the first place. They're known for getting things done, even in restrictive environments.

STORY: Jason

I approached my pastor one day with a strategy I had developed based on an idea that was floated around by the leadership team. I presented a product that would help our team be more hospitable, and he greenlighted the idea. I was eager to get started.

After approaching the rest of the team at the church—the ones who would help me make the idea happen—I began to get discouraged. Their systems were slow. The team wasn't willing to implement the project as quickly as I wanted it to get done. I felt like the project would take forever to happen, and that wasn't acceptable to me.

So I presented the issue to my pastor. I begged him to let me hire an outside company to help me build the product, and he agreed. He even authorized thousands of dollars for me to spend on it.

Well, the project got done, and it was exactly what I wanted. It accomplished my purposes.

But there was an unexpected side effect I noticed from my approach. By going around my fellow staff members to get the project done, I'd unintentionally isolated myself from them. I'd made them feel like my projects were somehow more important than theirs, and it broke a lot of relational ties that I had with the team.

Some people were more forgiving because I had better relationships with them. But it took me a while to regain the trust of some team members I didn't work with every day.

I had been so focused on the short term (the task) that I sacrificed the long term (the relationship).

The problem with work-arounds is that once we rise to the level of leadership, such methods can alienate us from our teams or hurt us in the long run. Yes, we solve an immediate problem, but we sacrifice long-term health. We might communicate to others—or even begin believing ourselves—that rules don't apply to us.

We can use work-arounds both internally—with our emotions— and externally. Most often, we resort to work-arounds as a reflection of improper priorities:

- In order to achieve perfection on this product, I won't work with a specific person, even though I need them on my team in the long run.
- In order to keep the peace, I won't have a difficult conversation with that person, even though it would save us many headaches down the road.
- In order to be perceived as right, I won't admit that I was wrong about an idea, even though I'll lose trust in the long run with the people who need to hear me admit it.
- In order to keep security, I won't do the brave thing God called me to do.

The more we make work-arounds a part of our daily decision-making, the more we compromise. We begin to isolate ourselves.

We begin to make decisions that will hurt us in the future. Consequently, a few months later, we find ourselves inheriting problems from our past selves that will lead to exhaustion and working far harder than we should.

Again, some work-arounds are good. As a leader with creative energy, you should be willing to cut through some red tape to get things done. But you have to choose your work-arounds carefully if you're going to be successful in long-term leadership.

The way to avoid negative work-arounds is to develop a picture of what you want something to look like in the future—family, finances, ministry, volunteer team, etc.

- What do you want the relationships to look like?
- What do you want communication to sound like?
- What are some future goals you want to accomplish in those spaces?

When you have a clear picture of how you want things to function in the future, you simply ask yourself if a particular work-around will lead you closer to that picture or farther away from it.

- Will "breaking the rules" right now enhance communication with your team or hurt it?
- Will taking the easy way out right now help you communicate better in the future or cause distrust?
- Will this shortcut help you accomplish the bigger long-term goal or make it more difficult?

Saving energy in the short term isn't always the best thing for you. You don't magically get more energy later. And choosing the difficult decision now—while you have more energy—can save you from having to deal with even more complex and tiring decisions in the future.

This idea is taught in toddler courses. Whenever a two-year-old throws a tantrum—say, because they didn't get to stay at the playground an extra five minutes—it's terribly tempting to give in to them. If you just say, "Fine, we'll stay," you'll stop the tantrum (maybe). The problem is, you've just conditioned that toddler to understand that tantrums get them what they want. Now every time you want to leave the playground, the toddler will throw a tantrum to stay longer. And even if you hold your ground for the next four or five times, the toddler still holds this thought in their mind: *It worked once, so maybe it will work again.*

Work-arounds that compromise your values do the same thing. In the short term, they're easy. But in the long term, they aren't good for anyone—for you as the leader, your team, or your organization.

Sunk Costs

One final note on values: Don't let past costs cause you to compromise your values.

There's a concept in the business world called sunk costs. Essentially, they save someone from making poor decisions based on past purchases.

Imagine a church bought an expensive piece of software a couple years ago. They've used it effectively, but now they need to make a change. Well, the software isn't conducive for that change, yet there's an emotional connection to it for the leader because they spent so much money on it.

The concept of sunk costs addresses the fact that money was spent and there's no taking that back. It happened. It's done. There's no redeeming it. And now the church has to move forward, cutting themselves loose from the bondage of that thing they purchased.

Now, sunk costs don't give you an excuse to be irresponsible with money. You should still research and plan expenditures wisely. But they do keep you from making poor decisions out of loyalty to something in your past that no longer serves you.

In the church space, sunk costs might be ministries you built that hold a special place in your heart. They might be systems you designed that took a lot of time and energy to create. They might even be decor that was donated by an important member of the church but no longer serves the purposes of the church.

Sunk costs are sacred cows that cause you to play a game of Twister, contorting your values and priorities in order to avoid messing up that thing from the past. Twister might be a fun game with trusted friends, but it's a horrible way to lead a team long term.

You have to be willing to let go of the past and press forward toward the prize (see Phil. 3:13–14). Avoid doing it in a way that destroys relationships or becomes an unhealthy work-around, but also don't let sunk costs keep you stuck in a system that no longer reflects your values.

STORY: Michael Turner, Senior Pastor at Advent United Methodist Church, Greenville, South Carolina

I knew that I needed to take extended time away to rest and be rejuvenated, but I didn't realize just how deep that need was until I actually did it.

In my denomination, pastors are encouraged to take a sabbatical every seven years. I have been in full-time pastoral ministry for twenty-two years, and only now have I finally taken advantage of that direction. I am five and a half weeks into a ten-week sabbatical.

Why did it take me twenty-two years? Because I felt guilty. Even when it started to become obvious to me that the cumulative stress and grief of the last few years were starting to take a toll on me, I was reluctant to talk to our church leaders about a sabbatical. I think my reluctance came from a couple of places. First, there was my pride. I didn't want to admit that I was bumping up against the limits of my capacity to handle the long-term, low-simmering anxiety and stress of the last few years. Second, we have some really gifted lay leaders who are extremely successful in the business world. I was scared that they would think, *I've been in business for thirty years and I've never had a sabbatical.*

Finally, I came to the conclusion that, no matter how anyone reacted, I needed to do this for my own health and longevity and that it would also benefit the church.

These weeks away are allowing the truth about rest to seep into my heart. The ministry of God's church, even the local congregation I serve, doesn't rise and fall on me. I've always known that in my head, but now the reality is settling into my soul. My new goal will be to fight the temptation to fall to the tyranny of the urgent.

God created us as integrated beings—mind, body, and spirit. We thrive when we are tending to our health in all three of those areas.

7 | FREE YOURSELF FROM ENTANGLEMENTS

Remove anything that can dampen your flame.

Have you ever seen a picture of a turtle that has lived entrapped in a piece of discarded plastic—maybe one of those plastic rings that holds soda cans together? Many times you can tell that they've lived for a long time tangled in the plastic, even growing into the confines of it. They're able to live and function. But they aren't functioning at their fullest. Swimming and walking are difficult. They can't get food as well as they were designed to.

Nature's ability to survive under less-than-ideal circumstances is pretty amazing. Yet if we aren't careful, we as humans can settle into these same circumstances. We can find ourselves in situations that prevent us from functioning at our fullest, surrounded by things that constrain us. They're physical or emotional entanglements that trap us in their hold.

For many, these entanglements often come in the form of addiction. Often when we think of addiction, we think of things like alcohol, drugs, and sex. If you're dealing with an overt addiction like one of those, stop reading right now. Seek a group or a counselor to help you get free. Pray and ask God to deliver you from the addiction, then get the support necessary to make that happen.

If you're entangled in an overt addiction, we want to give you some hope. We know you want to be free, you're frustrated that you feel powerless to do it, you're tired of feeling stuck, and you've been praying for freedom. We believe the missing component for you is bringing someone else into your journey. We break free from addictions through the power of help from others.

Though some addictions are obvious, many are not. They're secretive. They aren't as clear as addictions to substances or sex. For some, the addiction is to entertainment. Or ways of thinking. Or escapism. Or work. While those might not be as aggressive in their ability to take us out, they become constraints that entangle us and keep us from operating at our fullest capacity. They slow us down. They become a drag on us. They prevent us from doing things that should be easy for us.

STORY: Jonathan

Here's my confession: I have an addictive personality. This is largely the reason I stay away from some substances, because I can get addicted to things that aren't even known to be addictive. Now, I might not call them addictions. I'd call them obsessions. But whatever I want to call them, they're things that entangle me and keep me from operating at my fullest.

I've been addicted to coffee. To music. To puzzles. To games on my phone. Yeah, random things. And they aren't bad in and of themselves, but if I'm not careful, I can find myself thinking about them during the day. They begin to fill every amount of downtime I have. I even neglect work or sleep or relationships to pursue them.

For me, those things are forms of escapism, and I'm most prone to be addicted to them when I'm in moments of stress. If I get in a fight with my wife, I'm pretty quick to grab my phone and play a game. If work is particularly stressful, I escape to a puzzle or buy a new coffee brewing system and learn how to use it. You could call those things blowing off steam, but they're not just that. They hold on to me and keep me from operating at my fullest.

STORY: Jason

My entanglement is a bit more acceptable in the leadership sense. I get addicted to work. In fact, there have been times in my life when I've gone to bed at 12:30 a.m. and gotten up again at 4:00 a.m. I make myself so busy that I have to do this in order to accomplish all the things I've committed myself to.

In times of stress, instead of escaping like Jonathan, I find myself diving even more into my work. I take on more responsibilities. And I usually end up being focused on things that don't even matter, but the busyness simulates satisfaction for me.

We know addictions are harmful to us, but these smaller entanglements are sometimes just as insidious in the way they affect us. Big addictions will cause us to burn out publicly, but these smaller ones eat away at our ability to lead. They slowly and progressively dampen our fire. They do that by stealing our emotional energy.

For leaders, emotional energy is just as important as physical energy. There's a good chance your job isn't so physically demanding that your muscles are sore at the end of the day. You likely aren't breaking a sweat from all that intense leadership you're doing. Yet in the evenings, you find yourself tired because you're spending relational, thought, and problem-solving energy. That's all emotional energy.

Entanglements weave their way into our lives and eat away at the emotional energy we have to give to our work. That's where modern burnout comes from—not from physical exhaustion taking out our bodies but rather from emotional exhaustion.

The way you recharge your emotional energy is through rest. But entanglements prevent us from resting. You see this in gamers all the time. They spend three hours in front of a screen killing zombies with the smallest flicks of their fingers, yet at the end of those three hours, they aren't more rested. They're exhausted. The entanglement of video game addiction actually took a three-hour period that could have been reinvigorating and made it a further drain on emotional energy.

As for us, our two types of entanglements do the same thing. They both keep us from resting. The escapism, entertainment type simulates rest, but it doesn't actually give rest. It's similar to the video game scenario. And the other approach—overworking—just avoids rest, replacing it with frenetic energy.

We have to learn to rest—physically, mentally, and emotionally—if we're going to maintain long-term, high-capacity leadership in a healthy way.

So we ask you this: What are the entanglements in your life that are keeping you from properly resting? If you can't name them immediately, we'll help you by asking this question: Where do you go when you aren't even thinking about it or when you're stressed?

Do you reach for your phone to fill every bit of downtime? Do you turn on a football game and zone out for hours?

What fills your time? Or what stresses you out if it's left undone?

What about work things? Are you obsessed with keeping your inbox at zero emails? Does it physically stress you out if you can't make that happen? Do you need to check off every box on your to-do list and often work until late in the evening just to make sure you have nothing left undone at the end of the day?

There's a good chance those things are entanglements that have a hold on you and are keeping you from being able to rest.

Now, it's important to make a distinction here before we continue. There's a difference between entanglements and hobbies, blowing off steam, and relaxation time. Entanglements will simulate rest but leave you feeling tired. Hobbies, however, when used correctly, will actually recharge you. The big difference is that a hobby is a treat; an entanglement is the default. For some, video games are a hobby. For others, they're an entanglement. It's about how you use them. A hobby or relaxation time is something you schedule into your day, whereas an entanglement fills every empty space.

The problem is, hobbies and relaxation time can become entanglements if we aren't careful. Even those good things, when they get out of balance and begin to consume our mental space, can become entanglements. As the apostle Paul says in 1 Corinthians 6:12, we should not let ourselves be mastered by anything—even good things like food.

The telltale sign of people caught up in entanglements is the phrase "I'm so busy," but they don't have the schedule to back that up. They feel busy, yet if you were to have a twenty-four-hour view of their day, you'd see them doing something like spending a total of four hours scrolling through Facebook. It's wasted time that doesn't accomplish anything and leaves them feeling exhausted.

That's not the goal. The goal is more energy and less anxiety, and clearing away entanglements can help us get those. It can help us truly rest.

STORY: Jason

Can I be honest? Rest doesn't really appeal to me. I feel like in order to be a high-capacity leader, I can't disconnect for a few hours and get a massage or play a round of golf. I have things to do.

Still, my friends frequently send me articles about what rest looks like and feels like. Maybe I should take the hint. This is something I'm learning—what it means to rest as a high-capacity leader.

What Is True Rest?

As believers, we know the importance of the Sabbath day of rest. It's in the Bible from the second chapter and throughout. God even had the prophets chastise his people for not keeping the Sabbath day holy.

Still, we work. Incessantly. It's almost like we say to God, "You need rest. I don't."

There's always another email to answer. Another chore that needs to be done. Another emergency that needs resolving. And so we take the time that should be devoted to rest, and we work.

However, if we choose to embrace that restful space between work, we get

- Clarity. We can come up with simple solutions to complex problems.
- Physical energy.
- Emotional energy and excitement to return to a task.
- Creativity.
- More productivity. (Yeah, surprising, but it's true.)

STORY: Jonathan

For a season, I worked from a coworking space in downtown San Antonio. Parking was expensive, so I decided to ride the bus in. (San Antonio is not a bus-riding city, so my friends always looked at me like I was crazy when I explained this.) At first, riding the bus was frustrating for me, because it meant forty minutes each way that I couldn't work. I tried working on my phone, but that was always frustrating too.

One day I tried an experiment. I loaded into my seat on the bus and opened my phone to my to-do list. I just reviewed it, prayed, and thought about it. I organized items. I made a few notes here and there. And the craziest thing happened when I got to work. I finished my task list in about two hours—something that normally would have taken six.

Something happened when I sat still and just rested. You might say I was still working, but it was a restful work. I solved problems before they even came up because I wasn't so busy trying to churn through the work and actually let God speak into what I was doing.

When COVID measures shut down coworking spaces, things changed about my morning schedule, and I really missed the clarity that came from that forced space of rest.

If you're a busy, high-capacity leader, how do you find rest in the middle of the day when work demands things from you? Or when your spouse and children need access to you?

Disconnecting is easy if you take a vacation to Mexico, leave your phone up in the hotel room, and sit by the pool all day. But it's much harder to do when you're home. How do you enter into Sabbath rest when you're surrounded by demands that don't honor the Sabbath?

The key is to realize that a true Sabbath rest doesn't mean you don't do anything. The current Jewish practice of Sabbath isn't just sitting on a couch doing nothing. Jewish people tend to practice a form of active rest. They focus on something that is relational and energizing. And it doesn't have to be an all-day event. It can be a Sabbath rest in the middle of a Tuesday afternoon.

If you're going to find an active form of rest, you need to choose an activity that has your attention but doesn't own you—doesn't become an entanglement for you.

Walking, running, cycling, hiking—there's a reason these are such life-changing practices for people who institute them. They grab your attention but give you space to think. They give you space to pray. And in those times when you're praying, we want to encourage you to express gratitude for what God has done for you instead of just rehashing your problems while God listens to you try to solve them. The beauty of doing this during an activity (aside from quiet stillness) is that your brain has just enough to keep it occupied that it can't as easily wander to the things that stress you out.

The crazy thing about taking time to rest is that, while it constrains us, it can actually help us become more productive than if we didn't devote that time to rest. Parkinson's law is a humorous principle that says that work expands to fill the time we allot for it. So a busy executive writing an email might take two minutes, while a retired grandmother might take three hours to write that same email. One gets straight to it, while the other takes time to prepare her tea, get the lighting just right, organize the desk, reheat her tea, read over the email multiple times . . .

Rest limits the time we have to work on something, so it helps us focus on the things that matter most. It prevents us from doing unnecessary things while also increasing our productivity. Then, because we see forward progress, we have the emotional energy to work hard in short spurts instead of for long periods that feel like they drag on. Between those short spurts, we have margins for rest.

A crazy thing also happens when we slow down to rest—especially as it relates to emails. If we don't respond immediately to every email we receive, (1) problems tend to resolve themselves, and (2) people tend to be more thoughtful with their emails, knowing they won't play out like a text message. Yes, when we start taking time out of our day—intentional time—to rest, emails might pile up, but eventually the number of them reduces.

Intentional Time

True rest for a high-capacity leader requires intentionality.

A few years ago, Bill Gates did an ask-me-anything session on Reddit, and one of the questions was, "Can you give me a million dollars?" His response was so wise. He said that, while he would love to give the asker a million dollars, he had actually budgeted where every single dollar would go. He had decided at the beginning of the year who would get charity from his budget, and there was no room for anything else. Every dollar was accounted for.

It might be easy for those of us who don't have billions of dollars at our disposal to think that the rich have the luxury to toss money out the window from time to time, based on different whims. But the truly successful people who have money and keep their money are the ones who decide where every single cent goes—whether it's to be given, saved, or spent.

Now, imagine if we took that same approach with our time. What if we budgeted every moment of downtime with intentionality? So instead of just reaching for our phone during a thirty-minute break, we actually decided ahead of time how we would best spend those minutes. Maybe we'd take a walk or a nap or grab coffee at a new spot. We can plan our downtime to make sure we're using it for activities that are actually restful. This is the key to overcoming those entanglements that pretend to give us rest but only contribute anxiety to our lives.

Choose an activity that refuels you, and have it ready to go when you know you'll have some downtime. Maybe that means carrying a fiction book with you wherever you go. Or carrying wireless headphones so you can get into an audiobook. Or having your running shoes in your car so you can take a walk on a whim. Preparing for your downtime and choosing it intentionally will give you moments of true rest throughout your day.

STORY: Jonathan

A couple of weeks ago, I went to Universal Studios in Florida with some friends. One of my friends is an innovator at a large bank, and she's obsessed with the theme parks in Florida. In fact, she's an annual passholder at Universal even though she lives in Texas. She visits almost every other month. So she was the expert in helping us have an amazing time at the park.

She was telling me about a friend of hers who frequently goes with her. Her friend had suggested they move to Florida, working remotely, so they could go to the theme parks all the time.

My friend responded to that suggestion with such wisdom. "I go to the theme parks to escape and recharge. If I lived there, it wouldn't be an escape. It would blend my rest times in with my stressful work, and it would no longer be enjoyable. I actually choose to live farther away so when I do take time to visit the parks, it's a treat."

The beautiful thing about a trip like that is it has to be intentional. It's an intentional separation from the busyness of work so you can rest. But the same principle of intentional separation can apply even if you aren't going on vacation. You don't have to take a plane ride to another state to truly rest. You just need to intentionally separate, get your mind on another task, and give yourself space to rest.

Just like in soccer, basketball, and football, where players have to separate themselves from the chaos of the pack in order to make themselves available to get the ball, separating from the chaos of busyness gives you space to score. Separation from work might make you feel like you'll get less done, but it actually makes you much more successful.

STORY: Chris and Holly Brown, Pastors at The Well Church, Columbia, Tennessee

There's a tendency to numb ourselves. When our souls are tired and we're emotionally exhausted, it's tempting to just scroll or waste our time on Netflix. We do it in the name of self-care, but it doesn't get us there.

The best self-care we've found is tapping into the Holy Spirit, the only person who can actually energize us. The body tells us to numb ourselves if we don't like how things are going, but our spirits crave communion with God. We've become worn-out doing things in our own power, and we need to begin relying on the power of the Holy Spirit.

It's okay to pour ourselves out as long as we let Jesus help us find rest in the middle of it.

8 | ESTABLISH HEALTHY RELATIONAL BOUNDARIES

Boundaries help keep the right people close.

Consider this question: Who speaks into your life? Proverbs 18:21 says, "The tongue can bring death or life" (NLT). Are the tongues you're listening to contributing life or death?

This is an important question, and we believe it's never been more important in the history of the world than it is in this generation. Historically, the typical person had at most fifty people speaking into their life regularly. Those would be family members, coworkers, friends, neighbors—the people who'd have regular access to you. If you were a pastor twenty years ago, that number might have jumped to eighty because thirty of your congregants might have been regularly speaking with you. But the number was still low.

Now introduce social media and cell phones, giving instant communication with and connection to anyone anywhere on the face of the planet, and you easily have two thousand people who can regularly speak into your life. That's a lot of voices who have instant access to you.

Jesus told us to love our neighbors, which was already hard enough when those people were the fifty we regularly encountered. But the mission becomes overwhelming when we have two thousand neighbors. That's why it's more important than ever to understand what our responsibility for love is. As leaders, we need to understand appropriate boundaries we can set while still following the mandate to love those we encounter.

(Note: Helping people in need is not the same as giving someone regular access to you. We'll break down this difference a bit later, but we do understand Jesus's mandate to love your neighbor laid out in the story of the good Samaritan.)

Before we get into the meat of this chapter, let's entertain an idea. What if your love could be richer, deeper, and more maximized by setting boundaries? It's easy to think setting boundaries limits your love, but what if it actually refines your love? We believe boundaries will help you to love better.

Do you have a good sense of boundaries in your leadership? Or do you find yourself in one of the following situations?

- You get irritable at people's requests.
- You aren't dating your spouse because you don't have the energy to.
- Your kids frequently comment on your phone usage.
- People assume you're constantly busy and comment on it.
- You feel bad saying no.
- Your days feel like one emergency after another.
- You don't take vacations, or you feel guilty resting.

If you regularly see yourself in some of the situations above, there's a good chance you need better boundaries in your life. And if you don't start incorporating healthy relational boundaries, there's a good chance you're heading toward exhaustion.

Many of us, especially in ministerial leadership, are afraid of setting boundaries. Boundaries feel mean. More than that, they feel unloving, and we got into ministry because we love people.

It's important to realize that we aren't God. For God—not Pastor Pete—so loved the world. We don't have the capacity to love with the completeness that God does.

Boundaries help us create a framework for better loving people and for surrounding ourselves with people who recharge and energize us. In order to set appropriate boundaries, we need to realize there are three categories of people in our lives:

- get from
- sit with
- give to

There are people we *get from* who speak life to us. These are mentors, authority figures, and godly folks who have walked the road ahead of us. These people should have near-unfettered access to us.

Then there are those we *sit with*. These are our friends, peers, and others who encourage us but are also working through the same things we are. They have some wisdom, but they also require things from us. These are the people we don't always have to be "on" for. They should have regular access to us.

Finally, there are people we *give to*. These are the people we minister to. The contribution they make to our lives—if any—is the energy we get from serving them. These people should have occasional access to us.

When we have improper boundaries in our lives as ministers, the people who take from us have constant access to us, and the ones who actually mentor and encourage us don't have any space to speak into our lives. That will wear us out. But when we flip those two, it gives us energy to love better.

A boundary makes a decision between healthiness and un-healthiness. It doesn't mean we don't brush shoulders with certain people occasionally, but because of our boundaries, we don't do it regularly.

We don't want to hang out regularly with negative people. We do want to hang out regularly with positive people. However, nega-tive people aren't the same as people who make us uncomfortable. Sometimes some of the best people we can be around regularly make us feel a little bit uncomfortable. But they shouldn't be discouraging us. They shouldn't be impossible to please.

In the same way, not all positive people make us feel good all the time. Flattery feels good, but it ultimately will exhaust us.

STORY: Jonathan

I worked on staff at a church that my dad pastored when I first began in ministry. I was around twenty years old and still in college, and I felt like I was barely out of youth group. We had a youth pastor on staff who seemed fixated on me. He'd always come to me to "mentor" me. The problem was, his mentorship always led to my discouragement. He clearly wanted to be an authority figure in my life, and I didn't know how to deal with that. I assumed since he was a youth pastor he had to be *my* pastor.

I had the sense to discuss this with my dad, and he gave me some sur-prising advice. He told me, "You know, you're on staff too. Just because he's a pastor doesn't mean he's your pastor. You can tell him to back off."

And I did.

It surprised both me and the youth pastor. It felt uncomfortable. But that small boundary I set with him changed me from being discouraged almost every day at work to actually being excited about my job.

Some boundaries you might need to set with people in your life include these:

- *We will not speak about that topic.* Certain things like politics, past family events, and money will need to be off-limits. That's not from a place of denial—you should be willing to address hard topics—but rather from not wanting to keep beating a dead horse. Even Jesus told Peter, "Get behind me, Satan" (Matt. 16:23) when Peter tried to argue with Jesus that he wouldn't die.

- *There's a timeline for when I'm available to you.* There's a wonderful feature on your phone called "Do Not Disturb" that lets you set certain hours when phone calls and texts are silenced. You can choose people who bypass that boundary, but some people should not have access to you for certain hours of the day. Even Jesus went away to pray at times and was unavailable to people, often after a big moment when he was in the greatest demand.

- *There's a timeline for my response to you.* Some people need immediate responses, but some people can wait a day or two to get answers from you. You shouldn't be a slave to your notifications, and certainly not to other people's agendas, timelines, and expectations. Even Jesus stopped to heal someone while his friend was dying—he didn't let other people dictate his timeline.

You already have boundaries established in your life, though you might not think of them that way. Consider when you sleep. You likely have a boundary of not being disturbed between 10:00 p.m. and 6:00 a.m. That boundary is easy to keep because, mostly, our culture has it too.

Now, that doesn't mean that boundary is inflexible. If your child wakes up sick, you'll break your boundary. If a friend needs help at 2:00 a.m. because an emergency happened at their house, you'll gladly break your boundary. Even if a stranger knocked on your door at 2:00 a.m. because he'd been beaten up in your neighborhood, you'd probably help then too. There will be exceptions to your boundaries, but they should be rare. And if you find one person consistently being the exception to your boundary, it might be time to set a stronger boundary.

When we keep appropriate boundaries, we have time to let the right people get close. We aren't so busy being occupied with the wrong people that we don't have time for the right people to have access to us.

A boundary should be a gate, not a wall. People tend to build boundaries that are wall-like based on previous hurts in their lives. They keep people out. They're rigid. But gates allow people in, and it's up to us to open them to people. Gates allow us to protect what's inside, not just keep people out.

When we see a boundary as a gate that opens on command, we then have the opportunity to submit the opening and closing of that gate to God. We can let him, not people, determine the exceptions to our boundaries. And when God opens that gate after we've had it closed appropriately, we can be thrilled to make the exception.

If God tells you to fling the gate wide open and pour yourself out as a love offering, it is his calling, not the manipulation of others, to lay your life down. And God will be sure to sustain you.

Establishing Boundaries

Have you ever been on the other side of people's boundaries? Maybe you wanted to get instant access to them and something was blocking you. How did it make you feel? Did you perhaps feel a little bit jealous, like protection from unwanted interactions was something you wish you had?

Unfortunately, one of the dirtiest words in the leadership world is the word "no." People get mad when we say no, or, worse, we feel horrible saying it. But when we use the word correctly, it frees us up to be thrilled when we actually get to say yes.

We've both had difficulty saying no in the past, partially because of the way people phrase their requests. "Do you have time to help me with . . . ?" The answer is always yes. We can always make time. But it wasn't until we realized that our downtime is valuable enough to prioritize that we began to understand that we actually didn't have time to help. If we helped with that request (which was breaking down boundaries we'd established for ourselves), we would have to say no to rest.

Do you value your downtime enough to prioritize it as a valid use of your time? Are you willing to believe that movie you want to watch or that long lunch with your spouse is a valid use of your time? It is. But we so often don't realize it is.

We need time for family, time to recharge, time to eat, time to work out . . . Do you have time? Not if you're going to do the things you need to do.

So the first step in setting boundaries is valuing your time enough. But once you value your time, there are a few guidelines you should follow in order to set boundaries successfully:

- Never lie.
- Never avoid.
- Never omit.

Lying, avoiding, and omitting create a whole new world you need to maintain. When you do that under the guise of protecting your energy or time, you waste energy and time trying to maintain the false world you created. Instead,

- Be explicit about your boundaries.
- Approach them from a place of humility. "I need this in order to function."
- Offer alternatives. What *can* you do for the person asking for help?
- If you do want to help, expect motion from the other person. Let them do what they can so you can do what only you can.

STORY: Jonathan

When I was a worship leader at my church, parents frequently approached me, asking me to teach their children how to play the guitar. The first few times someone asked, I was eager to help, so I said yes. When I met with the kids, they pulled out their guitar, and I started showing them some chords and how to strum.

It quickly became clear that those kids had never even touched their guitar. And it made me frustrated, because a simple YouTube search of "how to play the guitar" would have done better than I was able to do.

Soon I began to respond to parents' requests with this answer: "Have the kids check out these YouTube videos, and once they've practiced what's on there, I'll be happy to meet with them."

Can I tell you? Not a single kid came to me after that. They weren't willing to do even a little bit of work on their own. So why should I waste my time helping someone who wasn't willing to invest minimal effort into the thing they wanted?

God doesn't help those who help themselves, but I do.

When People Get Mad

Won't people get mad when you impose boundaries on them? Yep. We can almost guarantee it. It might even mean displeasing the biggest giver at your church or your best-paying client.

That's why we need to stick with the knowledge that a boundary is good. Then we can use our gate properly to establish boundaries even when people are banging angrily on it from the outside.

The truth is, there are spiritual boundaries in life. God, in all his goodness, established a line in the sand. There are boundaries that can keep people from eternal life if they don't abide by them. And our response to that truth will determine the way we handle the boundaries.

Do you think it's right that your sin separates you from God? If not, there's a good chance you'll be mad at God. A lot of people are, whether they want to acknowledge it or not.

But if you acknowledge that those boundaries are just and right, then you get to receive God's exception to them through grace— amazing grace.

If people get mad at God, who alone is good (Mark 10:18), you have to realize that people will get mad at you, a fallible person, when you set boundaries. When you're willing to establish them, you also have to be willing to accept the consequences:

- You might get less done.
- You might make people mad.
- You might be perceived as lazy or resistant by some people.

You have to keep focused on the benefits of the boundaries, though. You have to remember that you'll experience

- more emotional energy
- less irritability
- better relationships with those who matter to you
- time to enjoy unexpected opportunities

STORY: Jason

Years ago, a friend I met at a church where I spoke invited me to Augusta National Golf Course in the off-season. We got to spend time on the course, go to the clubhouse, and get some free stuff. We also hung out with the superintendent. It was a once-in-a-lifetime experience I'll never forget.

The reason it was once-in-a-lifetime is because of the time later that year when that same friend called me up. He was a pilot, and he offered to fly to Atlanta, pick me up, and take me to play at the golf course. (If you aren't familiar with it, this is sort of the Mecca of golf.) And . . . I told him I was too busy so I wouldn't be able to go.

I didn't have good boundaries at the time. Had I proactively managed my time and boundaries better, I could have made room for this incredible experience. To this day, I still regret not going.

Nobody on their deathbed says, "I wish I could have gone to that meeting." They wish they would have experienced more things and embraced more of their relationships.

What if boundaries aren't to keep people out but instead are to help you give a better version of yourself to the people you keep in? When you're performing your best, you're giving people your best. You get to be available for those unique opportunities with people. It might mean making some people mad, but you won't remember those people at the end of your life. You'll remember the people and experiences you had.

When Boundaries Are Impossible

Now, we estimate that a large number of you who are second- or third-tier leaders have been saying to yourselves, "But what can I do when I'm not allowed to set boundaries?"

Perhaps your boss doesn't set boundaries for themselves, so they expect you not to. Or maybe your boss *does* set boundaries for themselves but doesn't allow you to.

We talk to many ministry leaders who feel this exact way, especially in ministries that are making a huge impact. But we might ask you one clarifying question before we continue on. Is it true that you can't set boundaries, or is that your own perception? Often we make assumptions based on what we see in people's public lives and build our lives based on those assumptions. We live a life free from boundaries because we believe (erroneously) that that's what is required of us.

So it's important to first find out from your leadership if your perceptions are correct. Here are some steps to start that conversation:

1. Be humble.
2. Assume positive intent from your leadership. Don't assume they don't want you to have boundaries.
3. Ask their expectations.

4. Ask for clarity on your perception of their expectations.

5. Ask what they think you should do to be healthy under those expectations.

6. Decide whether you can deal with those expectations.

Here's how that conversation might play out:

You: Hey, Pastor. I wanted to talk with you about something.

Pastor: Sure. What's up?

You: I've found myself a bit overstretched lately. I'm exhausted throughout the day, and I've even been getting a bit short with my husband lately. Do you think there's room for me to pull back a little bit to regain some energy and feel like myself again?

Pastor: I think so. What do you think is overstretching you?

You: One thing I'm doing a lot is responding to texts and emails after hours during the week and weekend. Is there room for me to delay response on those so I can be more present with my family?

Pastor: Hmm. I really rely on being able to get ahold of you. I wish I could plan my sermons earlier, but it just doesn't work like that for me.

You: I understand that. What do you think would be a good strategy for me to be more present in the evenings while still being available for the things you need from me? Do you have any ideas for me?

Then this is where we see what's possible.

If you have this conversation with your leadership, hopefully you'll find out you were perceiving things incorrectly. Maybe they do want you to set boundaries for yourself, and they expect you to take the responsibility for that. Or maybe you'll find out they don't want you to have as many boundaries as you would prefer, and you might have to change some things in your life to make room for their expectations. Or maybe you need to work somewhere else if you don't think you can maintain healthy, high-capacity leadership under those expectations.

STORY: Jason

I consulted with a church for a season when the leadership wouldn't allow their teams to set boundaries. Of course, they would never say it, but their actions indicated it. The way they operated communicated to their teams that they believed boundaries were an energy killer. They didn't want any limitations on anything from their teams.

I tried to help the leadership see that this was a problem, but they didn't fully believe their lack of boundaries was hurting staff, and they seemed not to know how to set boundaries for themselves. I saw exhaustion creeping in for every single person on their teams.

Hustle should be seasonal or in sprints. No team can operate long term on a constant level of hype. It's a guarantee of high staff turnover. Instead, there should be seasons of concentrated energy, followed by slower seasons for the team to recover.

If you find yourself in that situation but don't feel like you're ready to leave, your only strategy is this: Set boundaries when you can so you have energy to give when you don't have the ability to set boundaries. If most of your waking hours are spent at the church, directly in contact with your leadership, there might not be many areas to set boundaries. But this is where you need to operate under your values. Decide which priorities in your life are lower, and set boundaries there. Reduce negative voices in your life outside your

127

work as much as possible, and give yourself space to breathe when you have the chance.

STORY: Stephen Brewster, Worship Team Strategist

I was working at a church I had no intention of ever leaving. I loved working there. Unfortunately, a staff member made some poor decisions and wasn't honest about them. Worse, I was in an odd position of leadership because the staff member was also a close friend.

I found myself in a position where I was manipulated so that I couldn't be fully honest. I got pulled into conversations with the church leadership in which I found I had to hide things for the sake of the church as well as my friend. It was unhealthy, and I felt I had nobody I could share the burden with.

I don't feel like the church hurt me. People hurt me. Friends hurt me. But the church never hurt me. Understanding that and leaning into relationships has been a critical part of recovery for me.

9 | EMBRACE PEACE

Peace comes from less, not more.

Shalom. It means peace. But there's more to the word than that. It's a culturally important term that has endured for thousands of years for the Jewish people. It carries a sense of completeness, wholeness, being fully satisfied.

That's the peace we want for you. And that's the peace necessary if you're going to last as a high-capacity leader. Of course, that doesn't mean there won't be conflict. Shalom peace isn't about a lack of conflict; it's about a mental and emotional state despite what's going on around you.

It's the Psalm 23 type of peace:

> The LORD is my shepherd;
>   I have all that I need.
> He lets me rest in green meadows;
>   he leads me beside peaceful streams.
>   He renews my strength.
> He guides me along right paths,
>   bringing honor to his name.

Even when I walk
    through the darkest valley,
I will not be afraid,
    for you are close beside me.
Your rod and your staff
    protect and comfort me.
You prepare a feast for me
    in the presence of my enemies.
You honor me by anointing my head with oil.
    My cup overflows with blessings.
Surely your goodness and unfailing love will pursue me
    all the days of my life,
and I will live in the house of the Lord
    forever. (NLT)

Our culture places a huge value on information. Knowledge is perceived as power, and that power is perceived as peace because it gives us control.

But the truth is, we are no longer in the information age; we're in the over-information age. There's so much information that we can't possibly keep up, and there's a certain amount of FOMO—fear of missing out—that lives on inside our heads. That void of information is easily perceived as a lack of peace, so we search for more and more. But the void is never filled, and we never experience more peace.

Worse, if you're a teaching pastor or active in a church that values social media at all, you're expected not only to consume insane amounts of information but also to create it! That's information on information on information.

We believe too much information is actually the source of our lack of peace, not the solution to it.

We're probably about to be disowned by the leadership community for this chapter, but we think it's worth it if we can help you learn how to embrace peace.

There's a common saying that floats around in leadership circles: "Leaders are readers." And while we agree with that statement, we believe an overemphasis on reading is one of the main causes of a lack of peace among high-capacity leaders.

Before we get into this conversation, we have to bring balance to what we're about to say. Proverbs talks frequently about the importance of knowledge. It's wise to seek knowledge, and it's foolish to run headfirst into something without having any data or counsel to back our decisions. The problem is, we can have *too much* knowledge, and that's the challenge nowadays.

In the days of Solomon, information was hard to come by. You couldn't know what was happening a mile away, much less in another city or another country. You didn't have access to a thousand different opinions on the wise course of action for a battle or decision. You just had the people closest to you.

That's not the case now. Information today is more akin to the Tower of Babel. We've gathered everything together, and now seemingly nothing is impossible for us. But that limitless information isn't good. It leads to more confusion than to benefit. Perhaps it was never intended to be collected and centralized in the palms of our hands.

Could it be that all this excess information, rather than helping us, is actually causing decision paralysis? Having too many options makes it impossible to choose the "right" one when maybe there's no right one in the first place.

We do need information, but we don't need all the information. We need the *right kind* of information.

STORY: Jonathan

People assume I've read every book. At least that's how they talk to me over coffee. They'll reference a podcaster or author or pastor, then verify that I've indeed read or heard something from them. "I'm sure you've read _____."

Early on in ministry, I always felt dumb when I had to say, "No, I've never even heard of them."

Lately, though, I've become much more comfortable saying no. Maybe it's a survival instinct because the answer is almost always no, but I've realized I'm actually better off not having read or listened to every "expert" out there. I almost say no as if it's a badge of honor.

The truth is, usually these people bring up that author or pastor because we came to the same conclusions, and they can only assume it's because I heard the other person's opinion. But two people can come up with the same idea independently.

Have you ever been in that situation? Feeling incompetent because you haven't read the latest trending book or don't follow the popular pastor of the month?

It's an anxiety many driven people live with. It's the reason we have dreams, ten years after leaving school, in which we show up to school in our underwear or realize there's a test we haven't even studied for. We never want to feel uninformed. We never want to feel like we're missing out on something we should know. It's a fear built into us from the very beginning of life.

And now here we are asking you to consume less information. What?

Our society is all about addition and multiplication. Yet we believe the key to peace and better influence is actually subtraction.

The world says peace comes through knowing more, but could it be that Jesus wants us to know less? The world wants us to read more, listen more, watch more . . . But Jesus wants us to listen more to his Holy Spirit:

> The Advocate, the Holy Spirit, whom the Father will send in my name, will teach you all things and will remind you of everything I have said to you. Peace I leave with you; my peace I give you. I do not give to you as the world gives. (John 14:26–27)

Choose Information Carefully

We aren't trying to be overspiritual here and tell you to read only the Bible and listen only to the Holy Spirit. Again, the Bible talks about the wisdom of information. But we encourage you to choose the information you consume carefully.

Also, we want you to realize that there are rhythms. In Ecclesiastes 3:1–8, Solomon talks about there being times for everything. Just like there are times for planting and times for harvesting, there will be times for intense research and consuming tons of information and also times to stop researching and act. Be aware of what season you're in and respect it.

So how do you choose what information you should consume? These are the five questions to ask yourself:

1. Is it true?
2. Can I act on it in a reasonable time frame?
3. Does it pass the vibe check?
4. Does it encourage me to get back to work or make me want to give up?
5. Is it groupthink?

1. Is it true?

We've realized by now that not all information is true, right? And neither is all information actually information. In fact, much of what we call "news" nowadays isn't actual information; it's spin, agenda, and outrage.

How do you know if news is actually news? If you find yourself agreeing with it, it isn't news. Facts rarely require twenty-four hours of news cycles to be shared. But spin, agenda, and outrage rely on a constant rehashing of opinions in order to live.

STORY: Jason

A few months back, my wife began noticing a change in her day. She noticed her negativity and bad attitude in the way she interacted with people. That simply wasn't the norm for her, and she talked to me about it.

I asked her, "What's the one thing that has changed in your life that you think would make you start feeling this way?"

She thought for a minute and said, "I have been watching a lot more news lately."

It was similar for both of us, and we realized we'd both been feeling the same way lately.

So we reduced our consumption. My wife also asked me to stop contributing to the stress she was feeling by always asking her if she'd heard the latest news items.

And things changed. She began to have a better attitude toward people.

We aren't trying to hate on the news. In an over-information age, we crave things that tell us what we *should* know about. We want someone to curate the information for us. The problem is that they often go far beyond telling us news that's important to instead stirring up our emotions about a topic. Maybe we weren't meant to have opinions on every bit of news that comes our way.

2. Can I act on it in a reasonable time frame?

Is it possible to read too many books? We think it is.

Now, we know that runs contrary to all the conventional wisdom from leadership gurus, but something happens when we get over-whelmed with things we should do but don't have the capacity to do. We begin to feel like failures. We feel anxious. We feel inadequate for the task set before us.

The crazy thing is, businesses are growing right now that are meant to help us consume even more. There are websites that sum-marize ten to twenty books in the course of thirty minutes. How could we possibly act on all that information?

If a whole industry is growing up around the pressure we feel, maybe that's an indication of something that isn't healthy.

So ask yourself if you can actually act on the information you're gaining. If not, slow down. Maybe don't read that next book. Maybe stop after the first chapter and actually implement that thing you need to do, then continue on a month later. This runs against many type A desires to finish something once it's started, but over-information can lead to fatigue. And if you make this a pattern in your life, you're going to wear yourself out.

3. Does it pass the vibe check?

In Philippians 4:8, Paul tells us, "Finally, brothers and sisters, whatever is true, whatever is noble, whatever is right, whatever is pure, whatever is lovely, whatever is admirable—if anything is excellent or praiseworthy—think about such things."

Does the information you consume pass that vibe check?

It's far too easy to follow along with the latest scandal—a pastor has a moral failure or a massive church split happens down the street. Or maybe someone caused trouble in your church and now you're keeping tabs on them, waiting for the reaping to come from what they sowed. Don't get swept up in those things. You can be aware of them without being entrenched in them. You don't have to consume a ten-part podcast series or listen to twenty people tell their perspectives.

Scandals and failures should cause us to pray, "God, please keep me from doing that." Far too often we think, *They deserved that*. Pray for those people; don't evaluate them. Evaluation demands more information, whereas prayer trusts that God knows what needs to be known.

4. Does it encourage me to get back to work or make me want to give up?

There seem to be two types of experts in this world: those who want to help you get better and those who want to impress you with their knowledge.

The first type will encourage you and help you avoid blind spots. They'll make you better and empower you. The second type will overwhelm you with information and show you reasons why something won't work for you.

Whether it be a book, a consultant, or someone on Facebook, avoid information that makes you want to give up. There's a good chance you'll find a hidden agenda that might actually make the information harmful to you.

5. Is it groupthink?

There's value in thinking differently from everyone else. When Scripture tells us not to conform to the pattern of this world (Rom. 12:2), it's talking about the mindsets of temporal thinking.

And another element is at play: We should think differently because we're connected to the mind of God. His thinking is accessible to us.

Now, that isn't to say God will tell you the Greek definition of a biblical word for your sermon. You still have to do the research, but you'll get different thoughts when you choose to read something different from what everyone else does.

STORY: Jonathan

My pastor invited a guest speaker to our church. This guy's message was incredible. He had an example based on Scripture that I'd never heard before, and I'm a pastor's kid, so that's saying something. I remembered one particular part well because it had a poetic, rhythmic cadence to it. It stuck with me.

A week later, I was on social media, and I came across a video. It was one of those lyric videos for a sermon, and after about ten seconds, I recognized the message. It was the message the guest speaker had preached, almost verbatim. Except when I saw the credit on the video, it wasn't for that speaker; it was for a well-known pastor, Judah Smith.

It slowly dawned on me that the two hadn't independently created the same sermon but that the guest speaker had plagiarized Pastor Smith. I don't know why he would have copied such a prominent pastor or even copied any pastor at all, but he did. I lost a lot of respect for him that day.

Malcolm Gladwell, a journalist who has written many bestselling books on social sciences, has a MasterClass on writing. He has a few great quotes that apply to this idea of avoiding groupthink:

Google is set up to show you what everyone else is already reading.[1]

There's value in avoiding Google, because what gets to the top of the search results is the most popular content. If you want to think differently from other people, you need to be reading different things.

People assume if something is not current it's not useful. Nothing could be further from the truth.[2]

A wealth of knowledge is available from early church fathers and writers from decades and centuries ago that we just don't consume as much anymore. Older content might actually be better because it stands the test of time.

Why did you waste a week reading what was written in the last month when it's going to disappear?[3]

This is why it's sometimes best to wait a few years after a book releases to see if people are still recommending it. Many books are popular for a few months, but that's mostly just marketing. It doesn't actually mean the content is good. (Sorry to share the dirty little secret of the publishing industry.)

If you're a speaking pastor, this might actually be the thing that helps you sound fresh without having to overload on information. When other pastors are saying the same popular things as everyone else, you can cut through the noise by bringing knowledge and wisdom that have stood the test of time.

Now, this isn't something we're supposed to recommend as current authors, because obviously we wanted you to buy this book. We hope it was a popular recommendation as soon as it was released. But we also hope it stands the test of a few years' time so it actually helps people. We truly want this to be the book that helps people maintain healthy, high-capacity leadership for the long haul.

Still Small Voice

One of the greatest benefits of reducing the amount of information you consume during the day is that you make more space for God to speak. In 1 Kings 19:11–13, we read the story of Elijah standing on the mountain to hear the voice of God. Of course, the loud noises of the wind, an earthquake, and a fire passed by, but Elijah could recognize that the voice of God wasn't in those. His voice was the whisper.

The noises of all the loud information we consume seek to drown out the voice of God. But what we see in the story of Elijah is that he was so tuned to the voice of God that even the loud noises couldn't keep him from recognizing it. We can't always sit in silence, but we can train ourselves in silent moments to hear God's voice so we can identify it even in the chaos.

STORY: Jason

There's a monastery not far from my house. One day I took the opportunity to go there because I desperately needed a period of silence in my day. Of course, that's the rule when you get there: silence. So when I first arrived, I was nervous. It was so much of a departure from my normal rhythm that the silence actually scared me a little bit.

Tons of voices in my own head began to speak—voices of doubt, of anxiety, of desire for activity . . . It took a couple of hours, but eventually my own voices quieted and I began to hear the voice of God. Clarity and peace came into my mind. But it took quieting all the external stimuli that were so desperate to dominate my mind for me to experience those things.

We have the opportunity to stop things from filling our hearts and minds and to make space for God. When we have the opportunity for silence, let's not fill it with noise. Let's be intentional with the information we consume so that we can make room for God's wisdom.

STORY: Larry McDonald, PhD, Director of Doctor of Ministry Studies at North Greenville University

I was the pastor of a growing church. In fact, it was identified as one of the fastest-growing churches in the area. One day I noticed pain in my stomach. No matter what I did, nothing helped it go away. I finally went to a doctor, and they ran tests. I had an inflamed intestine—an ulcer. They told me I needed to reduce my stress, take meds, and be on bed rest for a week. My wife was pregnant with our third child, and because of complications, she was on semi bed rest too.

I didn't feel like I could take this break. Our church was in the middle of constructing a new building that would mean triple the space for our auditorium and double the space for education. I was also completing my DMin dissertation.

During this time, I studied Ephesians 4 and the ministry of Jesus with his twelve disciples, and I realized that I was doing the ministry, not training others to do it. I began investing in a group of seven people for seven weeks to begin taking more of the pastoral load.

It wasn't easy going. One week I was gone for an anniversary trip and someone in the congregation passed away. The men I'd invested in rallied around the family and showed them care. I made it back to lead the funeral, but the family had already been cared for by those leaders.

Some in the church criticized my efforts by saying I had favorites. It was about a year of people in the church not being able to adjust to the changes I was making. But I knew I had to make them if I was going to survive in ministry. I couldn't fear that I'd be replaced if I gave away too much of the ministry, because avoiding those changes would be unhealthy for me.

10 | SEE YOUR PAST DIFFERENTLY

Past hurts don't have to pollute your leadership.

You can't get through life without getting hurt. That's the sad reality of living in a community. People unintentionally (and sometimes intentionally) hurt each other.

STORY: Jonathan

I did the big no-no. I left my church. It wasn't because I was moving to another city, though. I was staying in the same city, just going to another church.

I say this is the big no-no because years ago, when I was working at a church, the worst thing someone could do was leave. Even if they left well—though more often they pitched proverbial grenades behind them on their way out—you'd always hear things a few months later about some issue they had with the leadership.

The leadership at the time I worked for that church? My dad. He was the pastor. Thus, anytime someone left the church, it ended up hurting me personally.

So years later and in our new situation, when my wife and I felt it was time to leave our current church, I felt like I was betraying people. Why would I do that to all my friends and family at the church? And my pastor—he was one of my closest friends.

The conversation was a difficult one.

"Jonathan," my pastor said, "I know you're telling me there are no offenses leading to this decision to leave the church. At the same time, I have a strong feeling that about six months from now, I'll hear the real reason you left."

Apparently, as a church planter and with years of ministry under his belt, he'd experienced the same situations I had.

At the end of our meeting, we promised to still hang out for coffee and lunch, and my wife and I began attending the other church. Six months later I was still saying good things about our old church, even while getting deeply involved in serving at the new church. Then a year later we found ourselves back at our old church.

It turns out I'm one of the few people who have ever left a church well.

Still, my pastor and I both went through the pain as if I had been leaving poorly. We both had sensitivities to people leaving churches because we'd been burned in the past. We had to relive past pain even though I was actually leaving in a healthy way.

Again, we can't avoid pain in this life—even in our church community. Sadly, church environments are often the worst for hurts. It's not because people are meaner and more inconsiderate in the church but because we get closer to each other in church than we do in other environments.

The guys you play pickup basketball with . . . You probably don't break down crying in front of them while you sing worship songs.

The girls you grab coffee with . . . They might not know how profoundly the difficult breakup impacted you.

We perhaps are more vulnerable with people in church, which opens us up to deeper hurt. Not only can they hurt us emotionally, but they can also hurt us spiritually.

If you're in ministry, you will bear most of that pain, because you're the one having to make decisions people disagree with.

Ministry isn't for the faint of heart. Ministry is exhausting and painful, but you already knew that.

The problem is, these situations that cause pain can add up. Sometimes experiencing the same situation just two times can lead us to develop sensitivities, which trigger us to think, *This is just like what happened before. Now it's happening again.*

Certain words, circumstances, names—they can alert our brains to dig up a past hurt. We end up reliving that past hurt even if the current circumstances are completely different, because we developed a sensitivity that's clouding our judgment.

Sensitivities keep us from healthy, high-capacity leadership because we respond to situations from places of hurt instead of doing what actually needs to be done in a given moment.

If we don't remove sensitivities from our lives, we begin to build a false framework for situations. That past wound becomes the lens through which we see so many situations. It becomes a philosophy about people, and it keeps us from seeing the truth of the situation. Sometimes we'll even be proven wrong, but that exception only proves our rule instead of causing us to rethink it.

Think about Jonathan's situation of leaving the church. Both parties assumed the worst about it and even lived the emotions of it, even though that didn't match what was actually happening.

So how do sensitivities form?

They start with wounds. And not all wounds have to be big. In fact, sometimes the smaller wounds are more insidious because we don't address them. We'll acknowledge massive wrongs that were perpetrated against us, but the smaller ones feel silly to bring up. Instead, we bury them and assume time will heal them. The thing is, time isn't a guaranteed healer. Sometimes time leaves wounds exactly the same. Sometimes it makes them worse.

Big wounds tend to get us to counseling, but counselors often spend the majority of their time dealing with the smaller wounds. The sum of those smaller wounds—since they aren't as obvious—leads to our dysfunction. And when we don't respond correctly to them (through forgiveness), we turn them into a sensitivity that colors all our interactions moving forward.

We guarantee you have sensitivities, but sometimes understanding what they are can be difficult. One way to identify them is to look for verbiage or thought processes like these:

- This always happens.
- People always . . .
- It's happening again.

If you feel like the same things keep happening again and again, it could be an indication that you're in an unhealthy environment that perpetuates dysfunction. However, it could also indicate a sensitivity that has grown in your heart and needs to be healed. It could be that you're misinterpreting many events that seem similar but aren't, based solely on small past wounds that have accumulated and built a sensitivity.

Perhaps your ability to lead clearly and effectively is getting undermined by the way you see the world. You might think people are

- untrustworthy
- lazy

- selfish
- quick to leave
- undependable
- fickle

If you find yourself nodding aggressively at any of those characteristics, it might be time to identify a sensitivity and remove it.

Overcoming Sensitivities in the Short Term

Getting rid of sensitivities is a bit of a process. Fortunately, you can do something right now to start removing these pesky things that can get in the way of you leading effectively: communicate with humility.

Sensitivities, which cause us to live through a hurt that may not be actually happening, function best in the gaps between communication. We make assumptions about people's motives or their future actions.

Assumptions are easy because communication is imperfect. When people are speaking with us, we don't know what questions to ask and they don't know what questions to answer. Or, worse, they act without any communication, and we're left trying to figure out the why behind their movements.

Whenever possible, don't let gaps in communication occur. If you find yourself moving toward a place of hurt, reach out to the person and ask them about their motives and actions. Do it humbly and without accusation. Use "I" statements instead of "you" statements.

If you've operated for a long time from a place of reacting based on sensitivities, this will be difficult. You'll likely feel a little bit foolish as you approach conversations. You might find the natural way to approach these conversations is by saying,

- "Why are you doing this to me?"
- "Your actions are hurting me."
- "You're acting foolishly."

But doing this sets people up as adversaries. It puts them in a place of defense, keeping communication from being clear. In fact, you'll likely be triggering their sensitivities, and nobody gets ahead when you're both operating that way.

Instead, approach the conversations with humility, which sounds more like,

- "My insecurity is probably causing me to misinterpret your motives. Can you help me understand your reasons for _____?"
- "When you did _____, I interpreted it this way. I understand that might be flawed reasoning. Can you help me understand what's going on?"

If you find sensitivities flaring up, don't just brush them under the rug. Humble yourself and acknowledge the opportunity for a small amount of healing. Communicate, even if it makes you seem oversensitive, and avoid assumptions about other people's motives and actions.

The more we begin seeing that people aren't operating in alignment with our flawed view of the world, the more we can begin dismantling those dysfunctional systems we've been operating from.

Reframing Your Pain

In the short term, you can learn to communicate to get around sensitivities that can hinder healthy, high-capacity leadership. But learning to forgive people is what's going to set you up to lead at a high level long term.

Sensitivities can cause us to misinterpret events as hurts, but what about when the hurts are real? There will be times after communicating and removing assumptions that you find out, *Oh, they really are intending me harm.* But you can't afford to let that derail you.

STORY: Jason

I once worked at a church where I had to learn how to forgive. An event happened that could have derailed my leadership if it weren't for counseling I received after the offense.

I had already worked at the church for a number of years, and my plan was to stay there longer. One day a member of the personnel committee approached me with a proposal. He wanted to get rid of the current pastor, but he needed help. He suggested that, if I helped him accomplish his goal, he could make me the next pastor of the church.

I recall him sensing my resistance and upping the stakes: *Either you help me get rid of the pastor, or, after I get rid of him, I'll get rid of you too.*

I was unwilling to help him.

I then had to sit in a meeting where this man yelled and called me names. And while that hurt, the sense of abandonment I felt from him was the deeper cut. He had brought me into the church, but now that I no longer served his agenda, he was casting me aside. It felt like a betrayal of me and a betrayal of what was right.

The whole situation affected me far deeper than I thought it would. I found I couldn't get past it, and I knew it would negatively affect my ability to lead in my next job.

So I saw a counselor. It's funny, because I needed only one fifty-minute session with him to be able to work things out.

Adam asked me a series of questions that helped me break from the emotional pattern that the offense had created within me. He helped me get some separation from the emotion and see the problem objectively. I realized that if I kept looking at it the same way I had been, it was going to cripple me. But if I was able to look at it in a new way, I could regain emotional health in spite of the situation.

I had to reframe the offense.

Adam helped me see that I hadn't done anything wrong. I had made the right decision to support my pastor, and I had honored the Lord by choosing not to engage in something that was unbiblical. I took responsibility for what only I could control and let go of the rest.

When someone wrongs you, you can't fix what they did. People can't undo what they did to you. And even if you were able to sit them down and have them listen to everything you felt, the injustice will still have happened. They might apologize, but that doesn't fix it.

The good news is you don't have to fix the injustice in order to be able to forgive. You can reframe it.

Now, it's easy to reframe the results. We do this all the time.

- He treated me badly, but I'm better off being out of that relationship. I deserve someone who values me.
- It's good that I was fired from that job because I have a better job now.
- Things have become so much more peaceful since that angry person left our church.

It's easy to dismiss a season and reframe it based on the results you're seeing. But that doesn't do anything to help the pain. In order to deal with the pain, you have to reframe the offense.

That doesn't mean you excuse the person who wronged you. That doesn't mean you suppress the pain. It doesn't mean you devalue what you feel. Reframing the offense is about acknowledging what's under your control, what's under the other person's control, and what's under God's control.

Reconciliation takes two people, and it isn't always possible. But forgiveness takes only one person. And as Jesus followers, we're called to reconcile when we can but forgive no matter what.

The story of Joseph is a beautiful picture of reframing not only an offense but also a season of life. He was sold into slavery by his brothers, essentially left for dead. And when those same brothers eventually showed up in front of him, there was nothing they could do to fix the damage they had done to him. They couldn't repay the years he had suffered.

Still, Joseph forgave—the only thing that was within his power to do. Then he acknowledged that what his brothers had done was evil—not trying to exact revenge or make them feel horrible but assigning their responsibility to them. He also acknowledged God's responsibility in the whole situation by saying that he intended their evil for good.

God never intends the hurt. But he takes the circumstances and intends them for good.

Reframing is a sort of compartmentalization, but the healthy type. It releases control of what isn't your responsibility. You pack those things into other people's boxes. You tape them up and put them away. Then you're left with the only part you can do anything about. You clear away the clutter so you can forgive.

By clearing your heart of those pains, you can find a lightness in your heart. You can regain emotional energy that was previously devoted to the hurt and apply it to your leadership.

Forgiveness is a process.

1. Acknowledge and name the wrong that happened.

Clarifying why something hurt you will probably require humility on your part. For instance, you wouldn't say someone was wrong for leaving your church. Changing locations isn't inherently wrong. Instead, you might acknowledge that they said hurtful things to others about you in the process of their leaving.

For many, saying "that hurt my feelings" seems silly, but if you don't acknowledge the hurt, you're setting yourself up to create sensitivities to innocuous events. Every time someone leaves the church in the future, whether they say hurtful things or not, you'll feel the hurt from that first time because you denied it.

The offense isn't based on your preference. We'd all prefer that people stay in our church. But the feelings of rejection, abandonment, or betrayal are what caused the hurt, so the things people did to contribute to those feelings need to be acknowledged and named.

2. Choose to forgive.

Feelings are beyond our control, but conscious choices are in our power. Some people even find it helpful to write out a specific statement of forgiveness to revisit when the feelings don't want to cooperate.

Here's a sample script you can write on an index card to remember your forgiveness:

> _____ hurt me when they _____. They were wrong, but I choose to forgive them.

3. Choose to remember with forgiveness.

The feelings of hurt won't go away immediately, and they will pop up at random times. Maybe you'll see the person who hurt you at the grocery store. Or you'll hear someone speaking well about them. Or you'll wake up in the morning having just dreamed about them. Then those old emotions will flare up as if the offense just happened. But that's when you remember your choice. You remember you have chosen to forgive them.

4. Don't discount the good you experienced in that season of hurt.

It's tempting, when people hurt you, to discount the whole relationship as a loss. But there's a strong chance that some sort of good was deposited in you from that season of the relationship. In fact, we've both experienced hurts from previous leaders but still quote them to this day. We don't discount the things we learned from them just because a situation ended badly.

It's human nature to swing from one extreme to the other. We think someone is either all good or all evil, but the truth is, we're all battling. Our flesh wants us to do unhealthy things, while our spirit is seeking health and godliness. Don't vilify the person who hurt you, and don't discount how God used them in your life.

5. Move forward in forgiveness in spite of your feelings.

If forgiveness is a choice that we make, it doesn't matter if the feelings are there or not. We forgive and then move forward in forgiveness.

STORY: Jonathan

My dad is a master at forgiveness. He was a pastor, and I had the opportunity to work at his church with him for a season. I saw countless people leave the church, pitching proverbial grenades behind them, and I saw him continually forgive and even bless them. (The majority of the previous points on forgiveness are actually things I learned from his sermons.)

One day one of the pastors on staff hurt me deeply. I had worked closely with him in his ministry, and he left abruptly to start a new ministry in the same town. It was basically another church, but he didn't call it that because it didn't meet on Sundays. This allowed him to encourage people from other churches (primarily ours) to attend without disclosing that he was starting a new church. In fact, he even sent an email to many in our church, asking for financial support as he started this new ministry.

My dad—the pure soul that he is—never told anyone in the congregation how badly the man had left. Thus, many in our church assumed he had my dad's seal of approval, and they began attending and giving to his ministry. Many of my friends eventually left our church, and I had a hard time dealing with that season.

I had a difficult time forgiving that man. I'd made the decision to forgive, but every time I thought about him, anger rose up. And I'm not generally an angry person.

One day my dad was speaking from the stage, telling a story of when he had a difficult time forgiving someone. It was clear to me that he was talking about the same person I was struggling to forgive. He asked God to help him forgive this man, and he had the sense that God said, "Treat him like you've forgiven him." My dad didn't want to because it felt hypocritical to treat someone like he'd forgiven them when the emotions weren't there. But he said two things helped him do it: (1) It's always right to do what is right, even if you don't feel like it, and (2) Feelings follow obedience.

I decided to follow my dad's advice. I began remembering the good that I had experienced under the leadership of that man. When people asked me if I'd heard about the new ministry down the road, I expressed the things I'd learned under him. I even visited a few months later, and while it was awkward, I found my emotions had begun to follow my decision. I actually forgave him. I reframed the hurt and forgave.

Forgiveness is important for three reasons:

1. Jesus commands us to forgive, through a pretty harsh story he tells in Matthew 18:21–35.
2. Forgiveness acknowledges that we have been the traumatizer just as often as we have been the traumatized.
3. Forgiveness provides a vacancy for the Holy Spirit. The only way for us to be made whole again after a hurt is to invite the Maker into the gouges people have dug into our lives. He fills the spaces.

The Symphony of Leadership

There's a reason we love well-crafted symphonies so much. They reflect our reality. We have moments of memorable, beautiful melodies we could call the theme of the symphony. Then we have moments of dissonance that intrude into the beauty of the song, reflecting the reality of our lives.

Ultimately, the beauty of the theme wins out, and it stays with us.

God is designing a symphony with our lives and our leadership. We will have brilliant, beautiful moments of melody when everything seems to be right with the world. Then we will have moments of dissonance that intrude into the beauty and seem to mess everything up. God didn't design those moments of dissonance—they're just a result of our fallen humanity. But we can trust that he will redeem them by bringing us back to the melody. Back to the theme. Back to harmony.

We are designed to dwell on the moments of melody, on the theme God is building. If we allow ourselves to focus too much on the moments of dissonance between the melodies, they can become the theme of our lives. They become the earworms that play in our heads throughout the day, and they will ultimately derail us from what God has planned for us.

Choose to dwell on the melody God is crafting with your life, and you'll be able to achieve healthy, high-capacity leadership in spite of those moments of dissonance.

STORY: Ken Carter, Executive Pastor of Adult Ministries at Southcrest Baptist Church, Lubbock, Texas

When I was younger, my two-year-old son died. That was painful and lingered in my life for some time, as you can imagine. But I chose a path other than bitterness. I had to confront, feel, process, and understand the hurt to move forward, which set me up to care empathetically for others.

This translated to one story at a church years ago. It felt like a member was attacking me. She was constantly after me. I had been thinking about leaving the church over the conflict. I'd had people come to me about things this member was saying. She was affecting my leadership. I went to her to apologize, even though I felt like she should apologize. Sometimes you must take on the burden to initiate a conversation.

When I confronted her, she was surprised. She thought I was going to attack her, but I humbly approached her with gentleness.

I never found out what she was mad about, but that doesn't matter. I always tell my staff: If you ever have an issue with someone, go to them personally after you have prayed about it. Don't write a letter. Talk to them face-to-face. Humble yourself enough to go to them.

11 | GO SPIRITUALLY DEEPER

There's no shortcut to depth with God.

Throughout this book project, as authors, we've challenged ourselves to avoid saying anything that ministry leaders have already heard a thousand times before. But in this chapter, we get to a topic that has to be discussed but has already been talked about a million different ways. How do we say something about spiritual depth that's new? You already know it's vitally important.

If we're going to maintain health as high-capacity leaders in ministry, we have to focus on taking our walk with God deeper and deeper. The sad thing is that nobody notices whether we've been spending time with God. Nobody really knows if we've been living holy lives filled with integrity. They don't see our prayer time. They don't see our self-sacrifice.

Except they do, usually quite suddenly. When things go wrong, when the pressure's on, when we're shaken, what has happened in secret suddenly comes to light. This happens in both positive and negative ways.

For some, a tragedy will hit, and the depth of their walk with God will be shown. They'll stand firm, praising the Lord, saying,

"It is well with my soul." But others will leave the faith completely. Their growing anger toward God and his people suddenly becomes apparent. The church, instead of something they're excited to build, becomes a hated place. The crazy thing is, these are the same ministers who have spent hours in the Word throughout their week. It's not like they aren't reading the Bible or spending time surrounded by the people of God.

If we aren't careful, we can begin reading Scripture and spending time around believers in our role as content creators, not because we're devouring the Bible for ourselves. Not because we're experiencing real life-changing community around fellow Christians.

We all run into this temptation of reading Scripture and wanting to take a quick break to jot down a note for a sermon or social media post. Our time devoted to God can quickly become research for our job instead of an opportunity to advance our relationship with him.

You know this. You likely struggle with it just as much as we do.

So what can we say about going spiritually deeper that you haven't heard a thousand times before? Nothing. You know what you need to do. We aren't going to make this chapter longer than it needs to be.

Take the extra time you would have devoted to a normal chapter in this book, and ask God to show you areas where he wants you to stretch your faith. Let him show you places where you've compromised integrity or right living. Schedule a recurring task on your to-do list to spend time quietly before the Lord, reading Scripture as a student, or praying for God to reveal more of himself to you personally.

There's no shortcut to depth with God. Nothing you'll read in a book will suddenly make it click. Relationships require devotion and time. But we guarantee that this will be *the* most important factor in your longevity in high-capacity leadership. More than that, this is what you were created for. When you walk closely in stride with Jesus, you fulfill your life's purpose.

12 | MAINTAIN HEALTH

Don't neglect the flame.

Now that we've come to the final chapter, it's time to share some reality about this book and the topic of healthy, high-capacity leadership. This isn't just a onetime read. Merely consuming the knowledge in this book isn't enough to set you up for success. If you plan to slap a Band-Aid on your leadership health, you're going to be back at risk of burnout in another year.

Just like James tells us to be not only hearers of the Word but also doers (James 1:22), you'll need to put these principles into continual practice if you want to be healthy in leadership for the long haul. You'll need to do some maintenance in order to keep going.

At the same time, we do hope this book has been a sort of reset for your leadership. We hope it feels like you just graduated from school with the eagerness to lead, back in touch with the thing you love about leadership. We pray you're optimistic and energized, ready to tackle any obstacle that comes your way.

Resets are important, but continual resets are what it takes to maintain energy. Fortunately, resets don't have to be tumultuous events. They can be simple.

STORY: Jason

My wife, Stacy, is a licensed professional counselor. When I talked with her about the notion of resets, she told me there are certain resets we can do to help us break free from unhealthy patterns like anxiety and negative self-talk. These are simple things we can do externally that actually change the downward spiral internally, such as

- holding something cold
- breath work (breathing in for four counts through the nose slowly, then breathing out of the mouth slowly for five counts)
- walking outside
- rubbing or tapping the chest (to reset the vagus nerve)

These seemingly insignificant actions can create a physical response within us that helps us break cycles of thought.

Resets break you out of an unhealthy pattern and give you the opportunity to form a healthy one. If you're going to be healthy in leadership long term, it's important to continually recognize these bad patterns, reset yourself, and work to create new patterns.

Depending on how long you've been leading, it's likely you've developed unhealthy patterns. That's just the nature of being a fallible human. And while change is possible, often what makes it difficult is that those patterns you've established over the years seek to keep you operating the way you always have. Patterns that involve other people can be much more difficult to change.

You can see this sometimes in parents with children of different ages. A father might have a combative, emotionally distant relationship with an older child growing up. That relationship often continues into the child's college and adult years, even after they are married with a family of their own. The unhealthy relationship becomes a pattern that neither can escape.

Yet that same father will have a younger child and be thoughtful and emotionally present with them. It makes the father seem like two completely different people, depending on which child is around at the moment.

The thing is, the first child and the father both changed. You can't live twenty years without changing. But the relationship pattern wasn't broken, so it persisted in spite of the other changes. The relationship didn't allow the people to fully change, even though neither of them liked the emotional distance or combativeness.

A pattern will always repeat and persist unless you do something to change it.

STORY: Jason

We used to own a farm. It was a huge plot of land—around 720 acres spread out across many fields. You could always tell where people walked through the field regularly because that's where the grass was matted down. If I wanted to create a new path to the pond, barn, etc., I would have to start it by trampling the grass elsewhere. Over time, the old path would disappear and the grass would regrow, then a new path would emerge.

That's the sort of approach you need to take for your leadership if you want to establish new patterns and break old ones. Psychologically, it takes about thirty days for a new neural pathway to form. That means you need thirty days of consistency to change the pathway.

For relational patterns, changing the pathway will require humility. That's the only way to start a new pattern and break from the old one.

STORY: Jonathan

My dad was amazing as I was growing up. He was emotionally and physically present. Even though he was a pastor—and pastors' kids are notorious for going off the rails—all his kids are still serving the Lord. He somehow helped us escape becoming another statistic of pastors' kids gone bad. I chalk that up to his humility.

One time I talked to my dad about a thing he did when he was angry. He would get frustrated and get a look. Then he would scratch his head, almost like a nervous tic. So even though he was patient with us and didn't let that anger get unhealthy, it was hard to talk to him when we saw those physical signs of his anger. So I told him about "the look."

Now, my dad came from an amazingly unhealthy situation as a child. His father was an abusive alcoholic who even tried to kill him and his brother a couple of times after particularly bad binges. So it would have been easy for my dad to think, *Give me a break. I'm ten thousand times better to you than my dad was to me.* But he didn't do that.

He took all us kids to lunch and said, "I've been told I get 'a look' when I get angry. Can you explain that to me more and help me stop doing that?" I'll never forget that moment when a grown, busy, respected man humbled himself and asked his children for help to become better.

And it wasn't a onetime thing. He invited us to continually point out to him when he was getting "the look." He enlisted us to keep him accountable and maintained that humility when we pointed it out to him.

Are you stuck in one of these patterns—either in relationships or just based on internal thought processes? If so, revisit the respective chapter in parentheses.

- Not having a vision. ("Establish and Operate from Values")
- Struggling with staffing challenges. ("Release Control")
- Snapping at a particular employee. ("Establish Healthy Relational Boundaries")
- Believing the worst. ("See Your Past Differently")
- Wanting to overly control. ("Release Control")
- Letting people access you at any moment. ("Establish Healthy Relational Boundaries")
- Information overload. ("Embrace Peace")
- Thinking, *It is what it is.* ("Embrace Imperfect")

Is there someone on your team or a structure in your organization that hasn't changed with you and is now resisting the change you're making to establish healthy leadership? It's time to disrupt that pattern. Identify the issue, tell people that you need to change it, and ask for their help in changing it. It will feel humbling (maybe even humiliating), but especially when it comes to a relational pattern, that intense humility is the only way the person you're talking to will believe you want to change—especially if the pattern has taken decades to establish.

The pattern has to change, and it won't on its own. Fortunately, the other person doesn't even have to accept that the pattern is changing in order for it to do so. In relational patterns, or cycles, A feeds B, B feeds C, and C feeds A. If you disrupt one part of the pattern, you stop the cycle from being possible. You get a different result, even if only one variable changes.

You don't have to disrupt every part of the cycle; you only have to disrupt the part you're responsible for. Changing the output you give to a person doesn't give them the chance to respond the way they normally do, thereby breaking the pattern. You have that opportunity.

So we ask you to do this: Imagine your leadership a year from now. Imagine you go on a twelve-month vacation and then step back into your office, into a perfectly healthy situation where you feel like you can lead at maximum capacity. What do you see? What does the situation look like? How do you feel? Who is there? What resources do you have? How would you know everything is right?

Now ask, What's standing in the way of that? Look through the list below and circle things that are standing in the way of your healthiest, highest-capacity leadership capabilities.

I snap at people.

I'm quick to get angry.

Things can't be good enough.

I'm never satisfied.

I'm not good enough.

I don't have enough energy.

I feel alone.

I don't know where to start.

I feel a lot of guilt.

I worry I will fail.

I don't have clarity.

My team won't let me be what I need to be.

Someone is standing in the way.

I get too distracted.

There isn't enough time.

I don't have enough resources.

I don't trust my team.

I feel like God's forgotten me.

I feel distant from God.

I'm worried my team won't stick with me.

I can't rely on people.

We're willing to bet the things you circled above are patterns in your life that you need to break. If so, you aren't alone, but breaking those patterns is going to take discipline, integrity, and accountability.

Discipline, Integrity, and Accountability

Here's the discouraging news about those patterns you circled. Even if you break them initially, they're likely to come back with time. Patterns, especially if they've taken years to build, will maintain a pull on you for a long time.

Alcoholism is a perfect illustration of this. While your tendency to feel like everything needs to be perfect, for instance, isn't quite as destructive as alcoholism, we can still learn what to expect because they're both patterns that are tough to break. Alcoholics must always realize that they're alcoholics, even if they've been sober for twenty years. The tendency to revert back to that unhealthy pattern will always be there, and wearing that "alcoholic" label is helpful in maintaining vigilance against it. It does get easier the longer the pattern is broken, but even at a low level, the pull will always be there.

The good news is, not every season will be as much of a fight. In some seasons, the pull toward the pattern will be gentler. In others, it'll be stronger. It's a constant fight, but there will be seasons of rest from the battle.

There will also likely be seasons when you'll give in to the pull and make a mistake. You'll fall back into the pattern briefly, but if you've determined to maintain health long term, you'll realize it and you'll take steps to get back out. As they say in Celebrate Recovery, a Christ-centered recovery program, keep coming back. Whether you've failed or succeeded, keep pushing into health. Don't let shame keep you from showing up.

The liberating thing about knowing you'll make mistakes—falling back into those patterns at times—is that it gives you permission to make a plan for when it happens. If you delude yourself into thinking you've broken the habit completely, it'll be a surprise to you when you slip. But when you anticipate it happening—not giving yourself permission to slip up but rather knowing the reality—your plan can help you recover faster.

Far too many slip back into the pattern and just accept that it has too strong a pull on them. But that won't be you, because you're committed to maintaining the health of your leadership. You'll deal with the pattern so it doesn't deal with you. You'll acknowledge it—give it a name—and take the steps necessary as outlined in this book to break from it.

We can do this together, as leaders in ministry, and break the cycle of burnout, moral failure, and toxic leadership in churches.

Discipline

The first step for breaking cycles will involve discipline. We encourage you to establish a workout routine of sorts to begin breaking your patterns. Establish a systematic evaluation of where you are in your progress. *Am I getting stronger in this area? Am I addressing the actual problem and not just the symptoms? What is my next step in breaking this pattern?*

STORY: Jonathan

My wife is a physical therapist. So whenever anyone in our family feels pains in their body, they immediately consult her.

I had been running for a season, and my knees began hurting. I told her about the problem, and she performed a few tests on my legs to diagnose the problem. It turns out that my hips were weak. I didn't know why that created problems with my knees, but I trusted my wife's doctoral-level education enough to believe her. (Also, it gave me the opportunity to make constant references to Shakira's song "Hips Don't Lie" to my Latina wife, which I'm sure she loved.)

She gave me exercises to strengthen my hips. As I lay on the ground to do them, she told me to isolate certain muscles. I'll be honest—I had no idea those muscles were even there. Immediately after, I felt sore in places I'd never even noticed.

Yet as I kept doing the exercises, isolating those muscles became easier and easier. I became more aware of them, and the discipline of the exercises helped me know what was going on in that area of my body.

This is such a perfect example of what discipline does. Once you expose a pattern, dealing with the problem can be difficult because your mind hasn't learned how to recognize it. But as you do the difficult work of isolating the "muscle" and working it, slowly you become more aware of it and have more control over it. You exercise your "noticer muscle" through practice, making it easier to notice a pattern in the future.

You will get stronger as you keep working on that muscle, but it requires discipline to start. You might not see results at first, but consistent discipline over time yields results.

Integrity

As the saying goes, "Integrity is doing the right thing, even when no one is watching." (The same goes for discipline.) Moreover, integrity is that right thing spread consistently throughout your life in every area. You can't have integrity Thursday through Tuesday and then take a break on Wednesday. That was the type of thing Jesus got upset about when he confronted the Pharisees. When it was convenient in their timetable, they acted as they ought to, but they were known to take breaks.

Just as alcoholics with any hope of sobriety must clear out their liquor cabinet at home, you'll need to get rid of entanglements from your life that would seek to draw you back into a pattern. Clear stuff out that would make it easy to return to your patterns. Don't give yourself an opportunity to "take breaks" from that discipline.

Can we be bold and say that some of you might need to get rid of your TV? Or put passwords that only your spouse knows on your computer? Or buy an old flip phone instead of a smartphone?

Radical measures are sometimes necessary to break out of old patterns and make integrity possible. Do whatever you need to make it happen. We guarantee the results will be worth it.

Accountability

Ministers, especially pastors, are notorious for being lonely. Perhaps they think people won't understand what they're going through, or they feel like they have to posture themselves a certain way, or they don't want others to have to deal with their burdens. Whatever the reason, pastors tend to process everything internally, using their own inner voice as their only form of accountability.

First of all, that isn't accountability. We need people in our lives who aren't impressed by us. Again, we don't want chronically negative people who are always trying to put us in our place. But we need people who will call us out on our self-deceptions. We also need them to be people who are trustworthy enough for us to know that whatever we tell them, they're going to stick with us and help us through it, not just blab it to the nearest person.

Second, we need accountability to people so they can help us process the things we're thinking. Our inner critic will most often destroy us instead of help us.

Do you have someone you can truly trust to talk to? Or perhaps you let self-talk tell you things like these:

I'm the only one who cares.

Nobody will understand.

I feel so alone.

I'm the only person experiencing this.

I don't have a choice.

Our enemy, the accuser, wants us to keep our thoughts, desires, and sins secret. He knows those things will lead to burnout. But when we bring them to the light, they can be healed. So bring them to the light, then have the integrity and discipline to dismantle the patterns that would seek to derail your leadership.

Steady Rhythms

Discipline, integrity, and accountability are the steady rhythms we need in our lives in order to maintain healthy growth as leaders, but at the same time, healthy bodies go through growth spurts. Growth isn't just linear.

STORY: Jonathan

I've had seasons of intense growth when I've launched a new company or a new product or written a new book with Jason. But most of my weeks are largely set on autopilot. They're filled with steady disciplines and rhythms that I do without even thinking about them.

I use an app on my computer and phone called Things. It's an elegant to-do list app that helps you organize your tasks by project, by week, by role—however you best organize your life.

I organize mine best on batch processing. Most of my steady rhythms are Monday through Wednesday. On Monday and Tuesday I come up with content for SundaySocial.tv, schedule stage designs on ChurchStageDesign Ideas.com, and write emails for newsletters. Wednesday is reserved for new projects that require more thought and focus. Then Thursdays and Fridays are largely reserved for writing projects or new ventures I want to try.

In the Things app, I set up recurring tasks to match that schedule. So each day, I have ten or twelve things automatically populated on my to-do list that I don't even have to think about. This also includes things I want to prioritize in my non-work life like devotional time, working out, buying gifts for my wife, texting her something romantic, etc.

I rarely have to decide what I'll do each day, because it's decided for me. That's the discipline. However, I have times of growth when I move everything around for a few weeks in order to make space for the intensity of a new project. The steady disciplines during normal times allow me to get ahead enough on my tasks in order to do this, so my life doesn't go into a complete upheaval during times of launching something new. Then I can fall back into the steady rhythms when the period of growth is over.

We are in a never-ending cycle of steady followed by a rush. There are even rhythms of seemingly no growth (though we are growing) followed by quick bursts of growth.

The problem with these times of intense growth is that they can disrupt healthy disciplines. It's natural for seasons to do this, but when we live in a constant level of intense growth and hype, it can pull us away from those disciplines for long periods of time, and that lack makes room for unhealthy things. We personally have seen the most moral failures within the church during extended building campaigns or other high-growth moments that have disrupted disciplines in the lives of the pastors.

If you're entering a period of intense growth in some area of your ministry, give yourself space to break free from rhythms for a season. But make sure it doesn't last too long. A month-long spurt is sustainable, but a year-long spurt is asking for trouble.

You need moments of intense growth followed by times of resetting, evaluating what just happened, and preparing for the next season of growth. When you begin to see your leadership life as a rhythm of steadiness with intermittent seasons of growth, you can build structure into your life and not let the hecticness of growth throw you for a loop.

How can you organize your life in such a way that the disciplines you need to instill in it are always there to fall back on?

Stretch Yourself

The beautiful thing about establishing healthy rhythms of disciplines is that it can actually cause you to be excited about spurts of growth. Instead of big projects being something you dread, you actually look forward to the change in routine.

When you have nonstop growth goals, it's exhausting. But when you have a growth goal to look forward to, it's actually healthy. A growth goal gives you a healthy target and emotional energy to achieve it.

We need to be stretched if we're going to maintain health in high-capacity leadership. Stagnation of faith, lack of learning, inability to try new things—these reduce our influence and cause us to be a hindrance to growth instead of taking part in it.

STORY: Jason

I had some health issues several years ago and visited a chiropractor for sixteen sessions. I also visited a neurologist. I wrongly expected the neurologist to give me some sort of pill to take, but both the neurologist and the chiropractor wanted me to do the same thing: stretches. They both informed me how healthy it is to stretch our muscles. It helps us heal.

Yes, it's uncomfortable, but a little bit of discomfort is actually healthy for us.

Along with the steady rhythms, one of the healthiest things you can do for your leadership is to regularly put yourself in situations that require trusting God. Choose situations that stretch you and your faith. Then, as you see God faithfully come through, you'll gain bursts of momentum that punctuate the steady rhythms of leadership. It's in that balance, along with rest, that you maintain health and have that high-capacity leadership you crave.

Throughout life, we're placed into new situations that stretch us and even scare us. As we grow up, we start preschool, then elementary school, then middle and high school, then maybe college . . . Along with each of those, there's a commencement—not just celebrating what we've already accomplished but recognizing the new and scary thing we're entering into in the next season of life. We take a moment to breathe and celebrate, then we dive into that next scary venture.

It's funny, because when we get older, we typically like to settle into a career and avoid those massive, faith-stretching leaps. The same is true in ministry. Yes, we want the church to grow. Yes, we want to increase our influence and try new things. But we rarely do things as drastic as what we went through in school. We wonder how many times we avoid big leaps because small movements don't require radical trust in God for us to accomplish them.

When was the last time you tried something that, if God wasn't in it, would have failed drastically?

STORY: Jonathan

In my hometown, a local church was entering a building project. They'd done all the things they were supposed to do in order to build up money to secure the loan. Yet they felt like God was calling them to stretch their faith. My dad, a pastor at another church in town, happened to be attending that church the weekend they felt like God called them to do this drastic thing.

In the middle of the service, ushers walked down the aisles and handed an envelope to every adult in the room. The pastor said, "We're in the middle of a building project, but we keep feeling like God is calling us to trust him. We believe in the power of sowing and reaping, so this is what God has called us to do."

They had cashed out their entire savings for the new building in $100 bills and gave one to each adult. The goal was for the receiver to invest it in some way, and it was up to them as to how to return it.

Can you imagine how much faith that required? The staff must have had many conversations in meetings about how bad an idea that was. Surely over half of the people would take the $100 and run.

Yet here the church is, twenty years later. People heeded the call and invested the money, ultimately returning more to the church. They got their new building. They launched campuses around the state. Not only did their obedience to God stretch their faith, but they were also able to watch God come through for them.

Do you feel like God is calling you to stretch your faith right now as you read that story? He's asking you to add a gigantic log to the fire of your ministry. Of your leadership. And it's scary when you do that. At first, the log seems to squash the fire, especially if the flames have gotten low. The log appears to be impervious to the flames. You think, *Surely adding the log was a bad idea.* Yet, as you tend the fire and you're patient, the log begins to catch and breathes new life into the flames.

Is there a figurative log God wants you to put on the fire of your ministry? Of your family? Of a side hustle? Of your team? Is there a season of stretching that God wants to give you to not only increase your effectiveness but also bring new health to your leadership?

You don't have to burn out in high-capacity leadership. It isn't inevitable. In fact, we believe you can lead in a healthy way that inspires other leaders to follow your model. That's our prayer for you. We pray you will burn bright.

STORY: Dan Reiland, Executive Pastor at 12Stone Church, Lawrenceville, Georgia

About fifteen years ago, our church was dealing with some complicated financial and land-use issues for the central campus building. That summer, my anxiety came out of nowhere. I experienced heart palpitations. I couldn't concentrate. I'd become overwhelmed just sitting at my desk. That continued for a couple of weeks.

Then in a meeting with some of our leaders, I broke. They had no idea what was going on, but I told them what I had been experiencing. After a long silence, they said, "It's been too much pressure on you and for too long." Then they prayed for me. Their love and kindness were healing for me in that moment. (I smile now thinking about how I used to say, "What pressure? I'm good.")

I called a brilliant counselor and am very fortunate that the anxiety lasted only about three months, then never returned. But I had to learn a few things. I had to learn to recognize stress and pressure, I had to learn I had limits, and I had to let God carry what I could not.

HEALTH HALL OF FAME

Jason and Jonathan want to thank some of the people who have helped them maintain health in leadership.

Jason would like to thank:

Stacy Young—Your support is sacrificial, consistent, and enthusiastic.

Bella and Jake—Your humor, love, and honesty are cherished.

My parents—Your wisdom is steady and helps me make wiser decisions.

Bobby and Debbie Roberts—Your love and support are helpful in my life.

Lance Martin—Your friendship and ideas make me better.

Jonathan Malm—Your writing partnership means so much to me.

Dr. Larry McDonald—Your deep care for pastors inspires me.

Ray Johnston—Your passion for people and pastors is contagious.

Scott Conner—Your belief in me is deeply appreciated.

Blythe Daniel—Your voice of reason is helpful.

Counselor Dave—Your presence and words protected me when church people were pummeling me.

The Baker team—Your efforts bring to life ideas and messages for others.

Jonathan would like to thank:

Carolina Malm—You bring so much clarity to the stress in my life.

My parents—Your wisdom and leadership have been such great examples for me.

My siblings—Conversations with you about church life and ministry are always revelations.

Joe Cavazos—You're a constant conversation filled with empathy.

Daniel Villarreal—You always bring a breath of fresh air to places where I might grow cynical.

Josh Engler—You've shown me what a pure heart looks like.

Jason Young—You're the Moses to my Aaron or the Aaron to my Moses . . . who knows which one is who.

Blythe Daniel—You're a fantastic agent who is great at bringing clarity to new projects.

The Baker team—You all are joys to work with! Five books down!

APPENDIX A

BURNOUT ASSESSMENT

We want to help you evaluate where you fall on the spectrum between burnout and health as a leader, so we created a free assessment tool. You can find it at www.dontburnoutburnbright.com. This tool will show you areas where you might need to focus your attention and will lead you back to this book to help. Feel free to share this assessment with leaders you know!

JASON'S SIX VALUES

Illustration by William Warren

NOTES

Chapter 1 Leadership Is Exhausting

1. Dr. Tim Elmore and Dr. Art Fuller, *Leaders Everywhere! Nurturing a Leadership Culture in Your Organization* (Duluth, GA: Growing Leaders, Inc., 2005), 52.

2. *Yellowstone*, season 1, episode 6, "The Remembering," directed by Taylor Sheridan, written by Taylor Sheridan and John Linson, aired August 1, 2018, on Paramount Network.

Chapter 2 Embrace Imperfect

1. Chris Thurman, *The Soul Care Bible* (Nashville: Thomas Nelson, 2001), 185.

2. "GETMO: Craig Groeschel Speaks on the Idea of 'Good Enough,'" Open Network, accessed September 30, 2022, https://openblog.life.church/gls19-day-1-craig-groeschel-getmo.

3. Orson Scott Card, *Shadow of the Hegemon* (New York: Macmillan, 2009), 163.

Chapter 3 Know You're Enough

1. John Powell, *Happiness Is an Inside Job* (Allen, TX: Tabor Publishing, 1989), 6.

2. *Talladega Nights*, directed by Adam McKay (Culver City, CA: Columbia Pictures, 2006).

3. Rebecca Webber, "The Comparison Trap," *Psychology Today*, November 7, 2017, https://www.psychologytoday.com/us/articles/201711/the-comparison-trap.

4. Christopher K. Germer and Kristin D. Neff, "Self-Compassion in Clinical Practice," *Journal of Clinical Psychology* 69, no. 8 (2013): 856.

Chapter 9 Embrace Peace

1. Malcolm Gladwell, "Malcolm Gladwell Teaches Writing," MasterClass, accessed October 12, 2022, https://www.masterclass.com/classes/malcolm-gladwell-teaches-writing.

2. Gladwell, "Malcolm Gladwell Teaches Writing."

3. Gladwell, "Malcolm Gladwell Teaches Writing."

ABOUT THE AUTHORS

Jason Young is a keynote speaker, an executive coach, and a consultant. He helps organizations develop emotionally intelligent leaders, build healthy teams, and create remarkable customer experiences. He has worked with Chick-fil-A, Ford Motor Company, Gorilla Glue, FedEx, and other respected companies. Jason has an earned doctoral degree in the field of hospitality. He lives in Atlanta, Georgia. Learn more at catchfiredaily.com.

Jonathan Malm is a creative entrepreneur who helps the church. His projects include SundaySocial.tv and ChurchStageDesignIdeas .com, which reach more than 70,000 leaders each month. Jonathan consults with organizations regularly on guest services and creative expression. He lives in San Antonio, Texas.

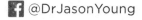 

§ **SUNDAYSOCIAL.TV**

A social media graphics library
geared specifically for churches.

Get instant access for
$10 a month.

Head to
sundaysocial.tv
to learn more!

Read More from Leadership Experts
JASON YOUNG and JONATHAN MALM